Vision in Action

SPIRITUALITY AND SOCIAL RENEWAL

· ·

Speaking, Listening, Understanding, Heinz Zimmermann

The Veiled Pulse of Time, William Bryant

CHRISTOPHER SCHAEFER

AND TÿNO VOORS

Vision in Action

Working with Soul & Spirit

in Small Organizations

SECOND REVISED EDITION

 Lindisfarne Press

This book is dedicated to SIGNE *and* BONS

Copyright © 1986 by the authors of the respective chapters,
Christopher Schaefer, Tỹno Voors, Stephen Briault,
Warren Ashe, and Roy Bunce.

This edition published in 1996 in the United States by
Lindisfarne Press RR 4, Box 94 A-1, Hudson, N.Y. 12534

Library of Congress Cataloging-in-Publication Data
is available.

ISBN 0–940262-74-6

10 9 8 7 6 5 4 3 2 1

Printed in the United States of America

Contents

Spirituality and Social Renewal

Books for a New Human Community

As human beings prepare for a new millennium, no area of activity calls out for more visionary thinking than that of social life, of community. It is the forgotten element in the scientific and technological utopia marking our century. We can build great buildings and cities, form multi-national corporations, develop sophisticated economic models—but we do so at the expense of the human beings for the sake of whom these things exist. The result is that our best efforts lead to an increase of human suffering on an ever greater scale.

We recognize that we have moved into a new globalism; that the world is one, economically and geopolitically; and that futurists extol the possibilities opened up by the new complex of silicon-based electronic interactive networks. Yet, at the same time, our thinking about who we are and what we are capable of as human beings remains pitifully inadequate and largely determined by nineteenth-century models. Thus all talk of "family values," of "virtues," of new forms of collaboration and cooperation, tends either to miss the point or to reinforce the most regressive aspects of our technology.

This series of books seeks to provide new social insights, perspectives of hope and practical idealism, based on a recognition of the fundamental spiritual nature of human and social life. It will explore how we can become more conscious and spiritually responsible creators of community and of a social and economic order which can serve the human future.

Introduction to the Second Revised Edition

AS INDIVIDUALS we are confronted with a host of societal issues over which we appear to have little control. The complexity of questions, the size of governmental bureaucracies, the inflexibility of the political process and the weight of everyday concerns combine to breed a feeling of powerlessness. Yet there is an area in which we can and do make a difference—the realm of initiative, of social creation. In the development of shops, educational centers, service institutions, volunteer programs, and small companies and in the transformation of human relationships our ideas and our acts do matter. The social world is a humanly created world. How an office looks, the quality of a product, and the manner in which coworkers talk to each other can be shaped and altered by our deeds.

This book is about the social creation process and is for initiative-takers, in fact, for all of us to the degree that we consciously choose to affect the social environment we live and work in. It is of particular relevance for individuals and groups who are starting or have started schools, shops, community projects, therapeutic centers, or small businesses and want to work on a cooperative, collegial basis. What it offers are principles, perspectives, and guidelines to widen the realm of choice and to encourage the will for taking initiatives that serve the spirit, the human being, and the earth.

Much of the content of this book was developed in a course on community development given at the Centre for Social Development, Emerson College, England, by both of us in the early eighties. It also draws on our experiences as consultants and facilitators with a wide variety of small- and medium-sized clients in England, Holland, and the United States. Modifications and changes in the content, sequence, and style of the second edition have come from the many helpful comments the readers and users of the book have made. We have been grateful for these responses and hope you will continue to let us know what is helpful and what isn't, as well as keeping us informed about your work. The revised edition contains two new chapters, one on development and fund-raising, the other on long-range planning. In addition, the book has been divided into three parts, Part I providing an orientating historical and philosophical perspective, Part II focusing on the practicalities of building and developing small organizations, and Part III describing opportunities for self-development and imaginative projects dedicated to a renewal of society.

We are indebted to the Community Dialogue Foundation, to the Rudolf Steiner Charitable Trust, and to Sunbridge College for providing the resources and time to make a revision of this book possible. We are also very grateful to our clients, to our students and their questions, and to our colleagues in the Association for Social Development for shaping the substance out of which this work has grown. May the wisdom and inspiration of Bernard Lievegoed (1905–1992), the founder of the Netherlands Pedagogical Institute and our teacher and mentor, accompany the efforts to develop a more equitable and healing society.

To encourage the taking of initiatives and the exploration of the ideas contained in this book, we cannot think of better advice than that given by W.H. Murray:

> Until one is committed there is hesitancy, the chance to draw back, always ineffectiveness. Concerning all acts of initiative (and creation), there is one elementary truth, the ignorance of which kills countless ideas and splendid

plans: that the moment one definitely commits oneself, then providence moves too. All sorts of things occur to help one that would never otherwise have occurred. A whole stream of events issues from the decision, raising in one's favor all manner of unforeseen incidents and meetings and material assistance, which no man could have dreamt would have come his way. I learned a deep respect for one of Goethe's couplets: "Whatever you can do, or dream you can, begin it. Boldness has genius, power, and magic in it."[1]

Christopher Schaefer,
Spring Valley, New York

Tÿno Voors,
Forest Row, Sussex, England

---

1. W. H. Murray, *From the Scottish Himalayan Expedition* (J. M. Dent & Son, Ltd., 1951).

1

The Historical and Organizational Context

1

The Human Being
and Organizational Life

CHRISTOPHER SCHAEFER

Our thoughts create our reality. The stronger meaning of
such a statement is that we are indeed co-creators of our
world and that ultimate cause is to be sought not in the
physical, but in consciousness.

Willis W. Harmon

The Historical Context

A hundred years ago there were few books on leadership, relationships, group facilitation, decision-making, or communication. Most people lived in fairly closed communities, in villages,
extended families, and small work groups. For many the world
was circumscribed by tradition, church, and family patterns.
People more or less knew how to work and live together, usually
out of tradition and habit. We had not yet become such a riddle
to ourselves that bookshelves could be lined with psychological
best sellers.

What has changed? What happened to human beings and to
society? While the answer is complex and has historical roots
going back into the Middle Ages and beyond, we can say that
today we stand at a point of increasing individualization, with
God-like powers over man and nature. Science and technology
have given us the possibility of preserving or destroying the
earth and ourselves. Religious codes, community norms, and
family patterns are less and less binding. We live in a culture in

which what "I think," "I feel," and "I want" are of paramount importance. This is particularly true of the "me first" culture in North America, aided by marketing appeals, images of instant gratification, and an educational system that tends to foster the values of taking care of oneself.

The positive side of this development is that we have the possibility of increased self-understanding and choice. What do I really think—what is right and not right? What values do I wish to pursue in life? What profession and lifestyle should I choose? There seem to be endless possibilities and choices, at least for those with the education and resources to pursue them.

We have achieved this increased freedom at a high price; ecological devastation and a growing gap between the rich and the poor, both individually and between countries. Equally disconcerting is the growing level of social fragmentation, isolation, and violence. How hard it is for each of us to understand a daughter, a son, a colleague, or a partner. We have increasingly become like hermits walking through the world, trying desperately to reach out to others, but ever less capable of doing so.[1] A riddle to ourselves, divorced from nature and isolated from other human beings, our modern onlooker consciousness is both a blessing and a curse. As Douglas Sloan has noted:

> The blessing is paradoxically interwoven with the curse. Paradoxically, it is precisely the separation, the abstraction, and even the alienation of modern consciousness from the larger matrix of life and meaning, within which human beings once lived as a given, that first makes possible the emergence of individuality and its singular potentials for freedom and love. The curse, or perhaps better,

---

1. See Rudolf Steiner, "How Can the Soul Needs of the Time Be Met," in *Some Results of Spiritual Research* (Blauvelt, NY: Rudolf Steiner Books, 1976).

the tragedy, of modernity is that abstraction, separation, and alienation came to be taken as the final realities. The result was assured by the acceptance of a sense-bound, abstract, and objectivistic way of knowing viewed not merely as one important way of grasping and understanding certain aspects of reality, but as the exclusive path to all knowledge whatsoever.[2]

If we can accept that there has been a change, an evolution of human consciousness, manifested, for example, by the development of psychology in this century, then a process of social renewal requires both a change in the structure of consciousness and a transformation of societal forms. We believe this is possible if three essential steps are taken in the process of working toward a more equitable and healing society.

The first is to replace unconscious social instincts no longer functioning in modern societies by a new form of practical social understanding, a social ecology that is not instrumental in nature and that recognizes the relationship between consciousness and social form. Such a social ecology recognizes that all social forms are created by us, are externalizations of our ideas and values and therefore of our image of the human being. Secondly, there is a need for us to develop ourselves consciously, to go on a path of inward transformation so that our consciousness is not only self-directed, but also capable of being outward-directed; of using our thinking, feeling, and willing to perceive others and the needs of the earth. It is a step of consciously learning to perceive the needs of the community and acting on this perception with morality and responsibility. Such a transformation is possible. It is the daily practice of interest and love. Lastly social renewal requires new social forms that enhance interdependence and collegiality,

---

2. Douglas Sloan, "Imagination, Education and our Postmodern Possibilities," *Revision* 15, no. 2 (Fall, 1993): 44.

that are nonhierarchical and service-oriented and that stretch us socially and morally.

Traditional hierarchical organizations divide people by level and function. I remember visiting a company in Bristol, England, which still had separate entrances into corporate headquarters in the late seventies for different classes of employees. The size and nature of such institutions either breed passivity or egotism and create high levels of alienation, isolation, and powerlessness. Smaller organizations that are managed in a collegial manner and in which goals are service-oriented and arrived at in common, encourage us to meet each other and our clients directly. They challenge us to develop a new social consciousness.

Increasingly, individuals, groups, and organizations are moving against the antisocial nature of the times, and of the modern mind set, by creating new life and work communities in which new social faculties are developed and in which the values of a sustainable society and economy are practiced. Self-directed work groups, consumer-oriented services, decision-making by consensus, involvement in mission formulation, ethical investment, and new forms of ownership are just a few of the emerging practices that are transforming the workplace and society.[3]

It is from our experience of working with many institutions of this kind that this book has been written.

Our aim is to offer perspectives and insights that will aid in the self-management of small, cooperative organizations, organizations that serve the earth and the human being.

The Human Being as an Image of Organizational Life

If we realize that organizations are created by people for people, then one of the questions that arises is: "Out of what model

---

3. See the quarterly, *CO-OP America*, for a description of such developments.

or metaphor are these institutions created? Is it an input-output model, a closed mechanical system, a biological metaphor, or a living image of the human being? We, like Berger and Luckman, think that all initiatives, all institutions consciously or unconsciously reflect the value preferences and ultimately the image of the human being of the initiative takers.[4] If this is the case then it matters what image is explicitly or implicitly chosen and what such an image tells us about organizational life and about forms of working together.

In the following section and the next chapter we will attempt to outline an image of the human being and explore a picture of organizations as living systems that reflect this image and, we believe, human nature. Such an exploration is meant to offer a perspective, an orientating framework, indicating the rough contours of organizational life, before we turn to the more detailed steps and approaches of how to build and develop healthy organizations.

While there are many possible images of the human being, our starting point is to see the human being linked to both a physical world and a spiritual world, while experiencing life psychologically through the medium, or on the stage, of the soul. This picture of the human being has been thoroughly and sensitively described by Zeylmans van Emmichoven, the Dutch psychiatrist, and can be checked against one's own experience.[5] In its most basic form, it does not substantially differ from that of Jung, Assagioli, or that of many humanistic psychologists.[6]

Van Emmichoven describes the soul as a stage on which we both experience ourselves and the world (both physical and

---

4. See P. Berger and T. Luckman, *The Social Construction of Reality, A Treatise in the Sociology of Knowledge* (NY: Doubleday, 1966).
5. See Zeylmans van Emmichoven, *The Anthroposophical Understanding of the Human Soul* (Spring Valley, NY: Anthroposophic Press, 1983), pp. 1–45.
6. See C. G. Jung, *Memories, Dreams and Reflections* (NY: Random House, 1961). Also Jung, *Modern Man in Search of a Soul* (NY: Harcourt, Brace, Jovanovich, 1983).

spiritual). Through our physical body we experience the world of matter and through our higher eternal being (ego) we are connected to the eternal world of the spirit. Our soul faculties of thought, feeling, and will (doing) allow us to both digest experiences and to independently interact with the spiritual, social, and natural environment. Seen diagrammatically, the following picture emerges:

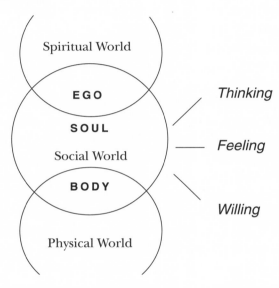

If we apply such a picture to our experience we know that in our consciousness thoughts are continually active, flitting in and out like butterflies: "Where is my pen?" "I really need to finish my cup of coffee." "What a strange sound." "Yes, I will stop for lunch at 12:30."

In our feeling life, things are somewhat less distinct: we feel a sense of ease and well-being when we are praised, irritation when we are interrupted, uncertainty when asked to do something new, or love and pleasure at seeing a close friend.

Our behavior, our will, can be consciously directed, but our underlying motives and direction in life are often hard to grasp: why do I fritter away time reading the newspaper or watching television when I have a report to finish or a telephone call to make? My subconscious impulses or drives often appear to be in a directing role. We seem to be most conscious of our thoughts, at least if we reflect, and least conscious of our drives and our behavior. In addition, we sometimes have experiences of grace—of important human encounters, of deep and abiding insights into life and of divine presence that are hard to integrate into normal consciousness. Some of these experiences are connected to the world of spirit and to our higher self, to our essential spiritual individuality.

This sketch of human nature is, of course, incomplete. It suggests we are beings of body, soul, and spirit, and that our psychological nature is experienced through the faculties of thinking, feeling, and willing. However, nothing has been said about the phases of human development, that incredible journey from birth through childhood, early adulthood, and maturity to old age. Here there are also aspects of development that we share with others: acquiring speech and the faculty of cognition, learning about values, understanding something of gender, coping with infirmity in old age. Talking with a fourteen-year-old girl is a fundamentally different experience from that of talking to an eighty-three-year-old woman.

While we share a threefold nature and pattern of human development with other human beings, we are also unique individuals, with the richness and diversity of each individual expressing itself in movement, tone, and the myriad details of the individual biography. As I often travel and sit in airports I observe people and try to imagine something of their life, of their universe. What a rich tapestry of human experience—the mother waiting for the son from college, the cheerful clerk at the cash register of the fast food establishment, the middle-aged executive checking airline schedules, or the homeless person in the corner of the baggage-claim area. Each shares the essential aspects of being on the earth, but experiences them uniquely, individually, with all the joy and sorrow that we are granted.

If organizations are an externalization of the human being and this picture of human nature has some validity, then organizations, too, must each have a unique identity, contain an aspect of body, soul, and spirit and have characteristic phases of development.

Three Dialogues in Organization

Given this picture of the human being and applying it to organizational life, we can distinguish three distinct realms of activity. One realm is the "body"—the building, the office, furniture, discrete work tasks, and the money received to keep the initiative alive. In a manufacturing organization this level of activity is the most obvious and receives the bulk of attention; for example, the making of engines, furniture, or lamps and the maintenance of equipment and buildings. In a school or therapeutic center it is less pronounced as the focus of activity is on the learning or healing process, but the bodily level is still important as it provides the basis for existence.

A second realm of the initiative is that of "soul," the quality and nature of relationships between people and the principles, policies, and systems that guide those relationships. How are working conditions defined? What salary arrangements are there? What is the style of leadership and communication? On walking into a store, college, or an office a mood can be sensed from the way in which people talk to each other, how they work, and how they view each other.

A third realm is that of "spirit," or identity. This level is difficult to describe as it is embodied in the initiative's culture, its vision, the needs it serves, the goals, history, and name. What makes the Barnabas Project in Detroit different from Shire Training Workshops in Stroud, England? Both work with unemployed youths. Why does one get a different feeling from one school than from another even if they are based on the same educational philosophy? The vision, the context, the people—

all of these certainly play a role, yet they only constitute the more visible expression of identity, of the spirit that lives in and through an initiative.

Each of these realms needs to be nurtured if the institution is to thrive. I remember going to a medical conference not many years ago and hearing a doctor say, "I ask every patient three questions: Are you on a path of inner development? Do you love someone? And do you like your work?" He thought that if the patient answered positively to two or more they were likely to be quite healthy. I pondered this for some time and realized that I approached organizations in a similar manner asking:

- What is the mission and purpose of the organization?
- Are the values, attitudes, and relationships in line with this vision?
- How is the vision kept alive?
- In short, how does the institution foster a dialogue with the spirit, with its essential identity, vision, and purpose?

I also realized that the question of do you love someone pointed to the soul life of the institution:

- What is the initiative's relationship to its clients or those whom it seeks to serve?
- What is the quality of staff relationships?
- Are relationships hierarchical and formal or informal and collegial?
- How does the dialogue between people take place—in what meetings, festivals, or conversations?

The question of do you like your work suggested the realm of matter, of task division, buildings, budgets, office systems, what I would call the dialogue with the earth in institutional life:

- How is the institution organized?
- Who has what tasks and responsibilities?
- How are budgets, salaries, and fees worked with?
- How is the life of the initiative expressed in buildings, color, work processes?

Just as we know out of our own life experiences that our total health is dependent on whether we are able to sustain a level of spiritual, psychological, and physical well being, so, too, is the health of institutions. Is the dialogue with the spirit alive, are relationships nurtured, and are work processes and finances given attention and worked with efficiently? These questions may appear simple yet they point to a number of important principles in institutional life. *One is that in the course of an initiative's biography these dialogues need to become ever more conscious if the institution is to remain in development.* In the early years much is intuitive and unconscious, but over time these three dialogues need to be consciously fostered if the bottom line, growth, or survival are not to become the main reasons for existence. Just as a middle-aged person becomes increasingly responsible for his or her own creativity and relationship to life, so, too, does the leadership of growing institutions. An unwillingness to engage in a conscious process of clarifying mission, values, and goals and in delegating increasing levels of responsibility when an institution has grown from 10 to 100 people over a number of years is tantamount to abdicating leadership responsibility.

A second important principle which emerges from this threefold perspective on institutions is the realization that, in collegial institutions characterized by limited hierarchy, the greater the shared clarity about mission, purpose, and values the less disruptive personality differences will be. The level of trust between people will be higher because, despite differences, we know we are committed to the same basic purpose. This in turn leads to a greater delegation of tasks and will engender more effective working relationships. Often when we get involved as advisors in conflict situations between individuals or groups and institutions, we find that there is not a clearly shared sense of mission and purpose. Conflicts then disrupt the smooth working of the organization that can then lead to poor performance and financial hardship. I remember one college that had grown enormously over its fifteen-year life, but the founder still signed all checks over $500.00, did all the hiring of administrative staff, and juggled their appointments every two years. The college, which included 600 teaching and administrative staff, was run like a baronial estate in which goals and priorities were not clear and leadership was not delegated. The level of discontent was fierce and conflicts rampant.

Seeing the relationship between the spirit, soul, and body of our own being and its expression in institutions, in the dialogue with the spirit, in the dialogue between people and the dialogue with the earth is an important aspect of building healthy organizations. It awakens us to an ongoing sense of which area of organizational life needs attention. However, in such a renewal process, it is important to remember that development is an extra, meaning that it takes place in addition to meeting all the ongoing tasks of an institution's life. Therefore, it is in weekend retreats and conferences and in a conscious self-assessment and planning process that these three realms can best be looked at and strengthened. Creating regular times for institutional self-reflection and renewal is essential if the organization is to be a learning organization and stay in development throughout its life.[7]

---

7. See Peter Senge, *The Fifth Discipline: The Art and Practice of the Learning Organization* (NY: Doubleday, 1990). E. F. Schumacher's book, *Good Work*, provides a rationale for organizations of scale, service, and sustainability. *Creative Work* by Willis Harmon and John Hormann (Knowledge Systems, 1990) discusses the changing nature of work and the role of business in transforming society.

VISION, ACTION, AND ACCOMPLISHMENT

by Gordon Collins

In working with organizations to bring about desired changes in their work practices, we have found the Vision, Action and Accomplishment model to be extremely useful. Basically, we are working with two dimensions:

- One dimension emphasizes an image of a human being from the threefold perspective of Head, Heart, and Hands or Thinking, Feeling, and Willing. Traditionally, business has emphasized the practical (hands)—doing and high levels of activity, and more recently the theoretical (head)—vision, strategy, work design, etc. What has been missing or in most cases dealt with superficially has been the "Heart" of business. The consequences of this are quite evident however in employee satisfaction, customer satisfaction, and ultimately the business's viability and economic results.

- The other dimension looks at action from the perspective of a "cycle of action" as opposed to looking at action as an event, something that someone either did or didn't do. The cycle of action becomes a context for looking at any particular actions (events) and allows us to ensure we are creating effective actions, implementing them and bringing them to a successful completion as opposed to just being engaged in high levels of activity.

By integrating these two dimensions we are able to gain a perspective that allows for a more complete picture of the human and organizational phenomena we are dealing with, from the redesign of business processes to the renewal of individual and team practices and actions.

Specifically, in our work developing managers as coaches we have used this framework to build new competencies for observing and assessing performance, and this in turn has provided us with a solid platform for effective coaching interventions aimed at developing people, eliciting commitment and achieving new levels of performance and results.

QUESTIONS—VISION

1. Is the vision expressed in a "tangible" way?
2. Is the vision coherent with our values, ethics, etc.?
3. Have we committed to the vision? Have we created an intention to act on it?
4. Is the vision providing us with an ongoing sense of direction in our day-to-day work? Is the vision "living" for us and being modified as we learn along the way to achieving it?
5. As we complete the cycle of action have we accumulated our learning and insight? Have we captured this learning in a process of continuous improvement and incorporated it in new ways of working?

QUESTIONS—ACTION

1. Are the actions we are taking consistent with our vision and intention?
2. Are the actions sufficient and coherent enough to accomplish the desired outcome/result?
3. Are there new actions we can be learning or taking along the way?
4. Is there energy and life in our actions or have they degraded into mere activities?
5. Are our actions aligned and attuned to any modifications in direction (vision) along the way?

QUESTIONS — ACCOMPLISHMENT

1. Have we created a context of accomplishment for the work/project at the beginning of the cycle of action?

2. Are we maintaining a sense of accomplishment in our day-to-day actions?

3. Are we bringing all three levels to completion:

• at the head level—is the vision completing itself in new learning and the accumulation of wisdom?

• at the heart level—is the context of accomplishment we created completing itself in a feeling of satisfaction both for ourselves and our customers?

• at the hands level—is the initial intention we created made real in the world, through the delivery of our product or service? Does it meet or exceed all standards of quality, expectations, etc.?

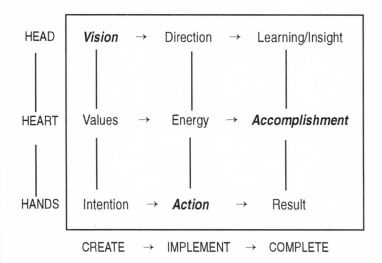

Gordon Collins is an organization development consultant living outside of Toronto; he can be contacted through the publisher.

2

The Conscious Development
of Initiatives

CHRISTOPHER SCHAEFER

We can learn to love, not only what is, but what is to be.
Bernard Lievegoed

The Nature of Initiatives and Organizations

Underlying this exploration of organizational and social life is the recognition that all initiatives and organizations are human creations, no matter how old and well established. They are created by people with an idea conceived in response to a perceived need, and they are continuously being modified by other people's ideas and actions. A school, a café, a company, may well carry something of the personality of the founders, but it is changed by the ideas and aspirations of those who now share the responsibility. So we live and move in a world created by nature and in a large and increasingly complex institutional world created by people.

As we have noted previously, this organizational world of banks, shops, restaurants, schools, and government agencies is one in which each initiative has levels of being, has a body, soul, and spirit, and, like a human being, goes through characteristic phases of development. Organizations are not mechanical systems, but, as Kenneth Boulding and others have noted, are *living systems* with phases of crisis, adaptation, growth, and development.[1] Consequently, organic metaphors such as seed, stalk, bud and flower, or childhood, adulthood and old age, are more relevant to the life cycle of organizations than mechanical metaphors such as input, output, clockwork or a smooth-running engine. One of the central tasks of initiative-takers is keeping the organization alive and developing it as a healthy living organism.

In working in schools, shops, and small companies I am frequently surprised by how little awareness initiative-takers have about their whole organization and about its stage of development and how relieved they are when they recognize that their organization, while unique, shares characteristic phases of crisis and development with other organizations. The following description is devoted to giving a general picture of the phases of an initiative's development over time, as an aid for individuals to more consciously shape and develop their organizations. The picture presented in no way seeks to deny the uniqueness of individual initiatives, but rather to describe the characteristic challenges and opportunities that exist in the life cycle of most organizations.

The Pioneer Phase —Improvising in Response to Needs

For an initiative to succeed over time there needs to be an individual or a group responding to a real need, a number of capable people willing to work hard, and some organizational and financial basis for the initiative. From the viewpoint of the life phases of an organization, one can say there is a gestation period when one or more individuals are walking around with

---

1. See Kenneth Boulding, "General Systems Theory: The Skeleton of Science," *Management Science* 2, no.3 (1952). Also, Gernier, L.E., "Evolution and Revolution as Organizations Grow," *Harvard Business Review* (July–August, 1972). And Richard E. Crandall, "Company Life Cycles: The Effects of Growth on Structure and Personnel," *Personnel* (September, 1987), for perspectives on phases of organization development.

an idea—an idea that is slowly ripening. This gestation period may be shorter or longer—often it is deeply connected with one individual's life and destiny. Henry Ford knew he wanted to be an engineer at age twelve. He also knew he wanted to found his own automobile company when he was in his late twenties. But it took him until age forty to finally create the Ford Motor Company.[2]

Following the gestation period is a moment of birth—when the school first opens its doors, the company delivers its first product, or the toy store has its first customer. This is a very important moment in the biography of all initiatives and it should be celebrated like a birthday. Usually this is done, often unconsciously, through a party, a festive meal, or even just saving the first dollar or pound earned by the new business. However, if this can be done consciously, as a foundation or a birth ceremony, inviting friends, customers, and helpers, it will help to get the new baby off to a good start.

Frequently I have experienced that the situation at the birth moment of the initiative gives clues to the characteristic challenges or problems an organization will confront in its life history. For example, a well-established school started many years ago with a group of experienced Waldorf teachers and a local headmistress who knew very little about the principles of Waldorf education. Its identity as a Waldorf school has since that time been periodically challenged by both teachers and parents. The Ford Motor Company resulted from a conflict between Henry Ford and his earlier partners. His and the company's relationship to the industry, and to the Detroit community in particular, had a troubled atmosphere for many years, in part because of this early rift. Another school I was once associated with was conceived and founded entirely by a strong

2. J. Westphal, "Henry Ford, Objective Idealist," *The Golden Blade* 31 (London: Rudolf Steiner Press, 1979). Also Henry Ford, *My Life and Work* (London: William Heinemann, Ltd., 1923), p. 23.

parent and community group without significant involvement by the first teachers. The result was that finding the right relationship between parents and teachers was a struggle in the school's history.

If the new initiative flourishes, it enters a period that is analogous to childhood: vibrant, exciting, full of surprises and of growth. Coworkers are involved in many activities, routine is limited, and the direction of the initiative is clear. It is a time full of ups and downs—a mood similar to the early twenties in an individual's life.

A couple who started a futon manufacturing and retail business a few years ago gave a picture that describes many early initiatives that have gotten off to a successful start: endless activity in deciding on staff, setting wage levels, ordering supplies, supervising production, keeping the books, getting bank loans, planning future activities, and occasionally stopping to catch a breath. They also mentioned two qualities essential to any starting enterprise: concern for the quality of their futon (cotton) bedding, and doing their utmost to assure customer satisfaction. The same qualities apply to a new school, a café, or any endeavor. Its reputation rests on the satisfaction of its clients, customers, or parents. If it provides a quality service or product, it will generally thrive.

Having a concern about quality and client satisfaction means that a new initiative, a pioneer organization, has to act like a large sense organ, continuously monitoring the satisfaction of those it serves while at the same time sensing how the initiative is functioning internally. If shop hours are not regular, or if a school is unable to maintain discipline, interest and support will begin to decline.

Sometimes people have the question whether it is better to start an initiative alone or together with others. In reality this is never an abstract question; a couple will decide to open a furniture store, one individual to start a college, or two partners—one in production, one in sales—to begin a manufacturing company.

In the past a single individual—a pioneer—tended to start a new venture and others then joined him or her, attracted by the personality and vision of the individual. Now, pioneer or initiative groups are more common. They need to be certain that they have a common vision and are equally committed with their time and energy. Absent and halfhearted initiative-takers are not readily accepted by those who are in it full time. Also the group should not be too large and should be capable of working together. If these conditions are met, then a group of individuals—because of its combined talents and wider set of human connections—has a greater potential than a single pioneer.

As the pioneer organization grows, it has a number of characteristic qualities that one can observe in organizations as diverse as shops, schools, companies, and therapeutic centers:

- It is generally of small to medium size, although I have worked with a community college with a teaching staff of 500, still in its pioneer phase.
- It has a shallow, flexible structure with a limited hierarchy. Key decision-makers are often involved in the full scope of organizational activities.
- It is person-oriented, rather than function-oriented. If you ask a pioneer about his or her organization, you will usually be told that Tom does publicity, Mary, craft therapy, Steve, counseling, and so on.
- Leadership is personal and direct with people generally knowing who makes what decisions. However, throughout the initiative's growth there is the need to clarify the role of the central carrying group in relation to specific task groups and supporters. Role clarification is especially important and potentially problematical in initiatives largely dependent on volunteer help.
- Decision-making is intuitive. Things are decided more by hunch or by feel than through a long process of

rational analysis. This style of arriving at decisions usually means that the pioneer organization is able to respond rapidly to changes in the environment. If you ask some of the early staff how they joined the initiative, they will tell you that they met with the key person or persons and more often than not talked about subjects quite unrelated to their field of specialization. One person I know was hired to establish a new psychology department in a college. He spent most of an hour talking about backyard grills and how best to build them, and was then offered the job.

- The pioneer organization has a family atmosphere about it. Everyone contributes as they are able, and most of the staff have a strong sense of loyalty to the founding group and to the initiative.

- Motivation and commitment in a pioneer organization are high.

- The goals of the organization are implicit—carried in the minds and personalities of the carrying group.[3]

This phase of an organization's life is exciting, somewhat insecure, and very creative. It is really about developing something out of an idea, a hope, and seeing it grow into an institution with services or products, a physical space, and staff. Another way of describing this is to say that one is bringing a child into the world—a child with its unique personality—full of vitality and potential. Very often one has the feeling of being helped, as if some entity wishes to have an abode on earth and is doing its best to make this possible. I believe that this is indeed the case and that developing an initiative is a process of providing the body, or sheaths, for a new identity to emerge.

---

3. See Bernard Lievegoed, *The Developing Organization* (Tavistock Publications, 1973). Republished by Celestial Arts, California, 1979, 51–61.

Consequently, the motives and aims of the initiative are important in determining what identity, what being is attracted to it. Seen from this perspective, the pioneer phase of an initiative is the time in which something of the identity, of the ego, of the initiative becomes visible, and the first home or physical body is created.

The Crisis of the Pioneer Phase

As the initiative grows, a number of problems begin to appear. These difficulties may occur five, ten, or even twenty-five years after its beginning. One of the issues is size; not everyone knows everyone anymore. New people join the organization in substantial numbers and do not share the joys and struggles of the early days, having no relation to the institution's past or the people who made it what it is. Another issue is that new structures of decision-making are needed to cope with increased size and complexity. Leadership often becomes unclear and motivation decreases. A sense of uncertainty, of crisis exists.[4]

In many smaller initiatives in the cultural and service areas this crisis of the pioneer phase includes some of the following phenomena:

- *A loss of confidence in leadership.* Increasing criticism, usually by newer people, about the "autocratic" and "irrational manner" in which decisions are made. Newer people have little relationship to the starting situation and the sacrifices that the original group made in getting things going. In some cases, these issues are also generational, with a new generation of people wanting both to have more influence and to work in new ways.

---

4. Martin Large, *Social Ecology* (Stroud, U.K.: Hawthorn Press, 1981), 71–74.

- *An unclarity about goals and directions that at an earlier time were embodied in the carrying group.* Then there was a personal relationship; if there was a question, everybody knew whom to go to. I remember attending a faculty meeting in an educational institution and watching all heads turn toward one person when a question of significance arose. In the absence of close personal relationships, the need for clearly understood goals and policies arises. What was implicit and personal needs to become explicit and objective.
- *The need for a definition of responsibilities and decision-making authority.* When things are smaller and more informal, one decision-making center is adequate, but if you have a kindergarten, lower school, and a high school or upper school, who has what responsibilities? In a college, what is the relationship between the teaching faculty and the administration, or between the departments and divisions? In a store, how will the purchasing, accounting, merchandising, and hiring be divided in an orderly fashion? Such questions become burdensome and, indeed, become the source of conflict.

In larger service and economic institutions, similar issues appear although often they focus on:

- more rational approaches to marketing and sales;
- rationalizing and centralizing staff functions such as finance, personnel, information systems, and marketing at the expense of operational autonomy;
- dissatisfaction with intuitive personalistic approaches to people;
- the need for more expertise, and more professionalism in production to cope with new technology.

In both large and small institutions the crisis of the pioneer phase is perplexing and painful. The need for change is recognized but its direction and how to achieve it often remain obscure. It is in such circumstances that a developmental picture can help, not as a prescription but as a rough road map so that at least the nature of the next landscape is discernible.

Differentiation: The Challenge of Diversity with Consciousness

The challenge of the phase of differentiation is: how can one move from the personal, intuitive, improvising mode of a smaller pioneer organization to a more objective, clear and functional way of meeting a larger organization's objectives. In my experience, there is a trade-off between consciousness and form in meeting this challenge. The more conscious people are of goals and policies—the direction and guiding principles of an organization—the less there is the need for rigid forms and control mechanisms. However, in the absence of shared goals and policies, hierarchical principles, procedural handbooks, and rigid reporting relationships seem to become imperatives.

Cultural institutions such as schools, professional organizations, therapy centers, and the like, often resist the pressures for greater functional clarity, attempting to muddle through. This tendency is quite pronounced in faculty-run schools, partly because most teachers have limited administrative and organizational experience. The trend in most businesses is the other way—replacing people by systems and so rationalizing operations that individuals may feel like a cog in the proverbial machine. The tendency to muddle through, to cling to a vague hope of the old unity, generates chaos and a struggle for power between individuals. The opposite emphasis subordinates people to logic and robs individuals of their creativity.

The central question for all types of institutions in this phase of development is to bring about functional differentiation without sacrificing human creativity and commitment. Achieving this balance, and entering a healthy differentiation process, involves paying attention to the following organizational needs:

I : RENEWING THE IDENTITY OF THE INITIATIVE

Renewing the identity and purpose of the initiative by developing a vision of the future and a clear mission statement. This means a renewed dialogue with the spirit, developing a vision—a struggle for the original and now newly willed central aims of the organization. The process of developing a vision of the future is akin to an individual's asking him- or herself what is really central to their life. It should involve many people in different parts of the organization so that a commonly shared sense of direction emerges.

A college I know took over a year to develop an image of the future and included faculty, administrators, and support staff in the process. While lengthy, it was time well spent as it generated a new hope and commitment. In many organizations suggesting such a process raises fears. Will teachers and administrators, or top managers and supervisors, not want totally different things? My experience suggests that such fears are unfounded. Generally, people see the same organizational reality and share a common picture of the values they want to pursue in the future. In a process of renewing the culture, the identity, of the institution, it is essential to also call to mind the initiative's biography, the rich texture of its history, personalties, failures, and successes.

II : LEADERSHIP

In conjunction with renewing the organization's sense of purpose, there is a need to create a new understanding of the different functions of leadership. What are the differences between goals and policies and where and how do evaluation and review take place? Such differences are seldom understood and yet such a differentiation in awareness, in consciousness, needs to be present to provide a healthy basis for differentiation in form and function.

While there are different ways of describing the main leadership functions in organizations, they often include the following aspects:

1. Goal Setting

2. Policy Formulation

3. Establishing Plans and Procedures

LEADERSHIP FUNCTIONS

4. Integration

5. Organizing and Executing Work Activities

6. Innovating and Renewing

7. Evaluating and Reviewing

Goal setting consists of setting long- and medium-term goals for the initiative. It is a central responsibility of those guiding the organization, although ideally those in less responsible positions should be involved.

Policies are different from goals. They provide a framework, a set of guidelines, according to which individuals can make decisions and act. Examples are policies on hiring or promotion, purchasing, sales, remuneration, and the like. This applies to schools and shops as well as to companies. If a hiring committee at a Waldorf school has an agreed-upon policy that Waldorf-trained teachers with at least a half-year's practicum are essential qualifications, then they have something to go on.

Establishing plans and procedures for particular work activities can be done if goals and policies are shared. The scholarship committee of a school can develop its plans and procedures if it knows what the policy on financial aid is and what restrictions exist in terms of the projected budget (a statement of financial goals). A small manufacturing company can plan production if annual goals and a marketing plan exist. In short, the delegation of responsibility becomes possible to sub-units, committees, or even to individuals, within a broad goal and policy framework. Developing such a framework is, of course, helped when the organization has already reviewed its sense of purpose.

The first three functions of leadership have been mentioned. They tend to be the responsibilities of all or most of the professional staff in smaller service or professional organizations. The fifth function, that of *organizing and executing work activities*, belongs to the whole organization, but the focus is on the worker rather than the supervisor. In a school it is the teachers or in a café the cook and the waitresses who need to organize and carry out the myriad of daily activities. Likewise, *innovation and renewal* are everyone's responsibility, although for the organization as a whole it tends to lie with those individuals and groups having a central leadership role.

Evaluation and review are usually understood as financial review and quality control in product organizations and are seldom paid much attention to in other types of institutions. Yet these activities are absolutely central to an initiative's learning and development. In schools or service agencies, in shops, farms, or medical facilities, they should be like an extended New Year reflection. How has this year gone? What successes and failures have we had? Why did things go wrong in this class or with this particular product? What can we improve upon next year? What new activities can we engage in? Questions of this type are vital, and the more members of an organization are engaged in answering them the more responsible the whole work community becomes.

The fourth function mentioned, that of *integration*, is like five, six, and seven; everyone's concern, yet it tends to fall heavily on those having a supervisory function. They must relate more general goals and principles to specific tasks.

Bringing about an awareness of the leadership functions in an organization is by itself not enough—they must be exercised. Where and by whom are long- and medium-term goals set? How are they communicated and responded to by other parts of the organization? I have worked with some clients where goals were set but planning was largely a paper exercise for outside consumption, and people within the initiative knew little about it.

Policy formulation is equally important. Where and by whom are policies to be defined? Plans and procedures are established and carried out in many parts of an organization, as are the other functions, yet what is important is that people are aware of what functions of leadership are being exercised by whom and how the results are communicated to the rest of the institution.

If we step back from this functional description and ask what really lies behind the differentiation process in organizations, then we can say that the soul of the organization is being developed. It is similar to what people meet in their thirties. There is work, the raising of a family, marriage, the garden, the mortgage, shopping, and finding some time for oneself. The challenge is to organize consciously, but in such a way that you do not lose life. Such a process of organization and differentiation is difficult for many initiatives because it involves task specialization and professionalization. But if the overall goals and policies are shared by people, then the conscious division of tasks can take place so that the whole benefits.

III : FUNCTIONAL SPECIALIZATION AND MANDATES

A third organizational need in the differentiation stage is that of functional specialization and structural clarity. In self-administered schools there is a need to differentiate the upper or high school from the lower grades and from the preschool. Administration, records, accounting, fund-raising, and publicity activities need to be consciously picked up. Committees need to be established as everything can no longer be decided and implemented by one decision-making group. In my experience, the following types of functions need the attention of individuals or small groups in schools and other cultural initiatives:

1. Curriculum Review and Planning
2. Festivals and Special Events
3. Hiring
4. Teacher Evaluation
5. Enrollment
6. Fund-Raising
7. Finance and Budget
8. Buildings and Grounds
9. Publicity

This list is by no means exhaustive, as there are schools with twelve or more committees, not counting the board and the faculty meeting.

What is true for schools is also true for shops, curative homes, therapy centers, and the like. The phase of differentiation can also be called an administrative phase, in which what was done semiconsciously to make things run in the early years now needs conscious attention.

An important principle during this phase of development is that of giving clear mandates and responsibilities to subgroups or committees of an initiative. This means that each committee needs to have clear terms of reference regarding the tenure and areas of responsibility. What often happens in self-administered initiatives is that committees are set up but that central decision-making groups have not established policies and are not really willing to delegate. Consequently issues that should be decided by the committee are continuously brought back to the central group and a process of second-guessing and criticism takes place. Discipline and clarity are required to establish and stick to mandates. Without such clarity and discipline, "republican" leadership, which Ernst Lehrs, among others, has argued for persuasively, is not possible.[5]

The need for specialization and functional clarity is even greater in product organizations. While in the pioneering stage marketing, sales, production, technical innovation, and finance may have been handled by a partnership of two or three people, later such a combining of functions is no longer adequate. Marketing and finance, to name two examples, are important areas of specialization in their own right and require professionals with support staff to be handled adequately. The same is true of personnel, information systems, shipping, purchasing, and a host of other areas. In addition to operating line responsibilities, staff functions need to be developed to provide the expertise necessary for the organization to function effectively. Here, too, clarity of policies and procedures allows differentiation without excessive control.

IV . A CHANGE IN LEADERSHIP AND DECISION-MAKING STYLES

If the above-mentioned needs of renewed purpose, new leadership functions, clear structures, and new style have been met, then an organization can enter a healthy differentiation process in which new functional structures are balanced by a new and different consciousness. The organization will then manifest the following characteristics, while still making an appeal to human creativity and involvement:

---

5. Ernst Lehrs, *Republican, Not Democratic,* occasional paper available from the Rudolf Steiner Schools Fellowship, c/o Emerson College, Forest Row, Sussex, England, and the Association of Waldorf Schools in North America (AWSNA), Fair Oaks, CA.

1. Increased Size
2. Clearer Policies and Procedures
3. Differentiated Structures and Mandates
4. A Higher Level of Professionalism
5. More Functional Rather than Personal Leadership
6. More Rational, Analytical Decision-Making
7. Greater Clarity of Work Activities

Institutions may develop and refine differentiated forms and procedures for many years, sometimes employing the latest technology in doing so. This period is analogous to middle adulthood and carries an orientation appropriate to the period of 28–35 in an individual's biography. Planning and rational analysis are most pronounced in this period of life, and in the "differentiated organization." As one would also expect, many people in their thirties feel more at home in this type of organizational environment than in the riskier pioneer institution.

As with the thirty-year-old, a differentiated organization runs the risk of too much rationality. The need for social contact, for a fostering of human relationships is very important. Can the staff of a well-established school continue with the vitality of spiritual work and create regular opportunities for meeting, for sharing meals, for knowing each other? Can a group of architects or workers in a shop create possibilities for the soul of the initiative to live? Soul differentiation needs to be balanced by conscious attention to "ensoulment," to fun, as well as work.

Many organizations reach this phase in their life cycle, often unconsciously and with great struggle. Yet it is clear that this phase too has its limitations, its period of crisis, as anyone who has worked in a large corporation or a big state institution knows. This crisis is most visible in those institutions where differentiation has been carried through by mechanistic structures, systems, and procedures without considering their impact on human capacities or motivation. In these types of institutions a marked loss of vitality, decreased motivation, high levels of absenteeism, and continued communication difficulties are evident.[6] While symptoms of this crisis are clearest in large bureaucracies and many companies in traditional manufacturing sectors, they also appear in smaller initiatives that have been in the differentiation phase for some time. The weight of the past, endless committee meetings, a lack of purpose, and limited innovation are symptoms that become evident in well-established schools, hospitals, and smaller retail companies. Being well established and, in most cases, quite secure, it is as if they, too, were experiencing a kind of mid-life crisis, searching for new meanings and a new way of working.

The interest in cooperative and associative models, in Japanese management forms, and in the qualities of excellence suggests that there is a conscious and widespread search underway in Western societies for possible answers to the crisis of differentiation.[7] The critiques of the Harvard Business School and similar institutions, and the widespread focus on new entrepreneurship—rather than the rational model—is another manifestation of this search for a new set of organizational principles. There are as yet no definitive answers, and, I believe, no one organization that offers the model for the future, but a direction and some new principles are visible.

The Integration Phase: Creating a Responsive Process Organization

In their best-selling book, *In Search of Excellence*, Peters and Waterman pointed to a number of basic qualities that have made some mature American companies successful. These include:

---

6. See Lievegoed, *The Developing Organization*, 71–76. Also Large, *Social Ecology*.
7. See T. J. Peters and R. H. Waterman, Jr., *In Search of Excellence: Lessons from America's Best Run Companies* (Warner Books Edition, 1982), 29–55. Also J. Naisbitt, *Megatrends* (Warner Books, 1982), 103–140, 211–231.

1. Clear-cut goals and a culture of commitment and excellence
2. Treating people as people and valuing their contribution
3. A decentralized and flat structure
4. An awareness of the central work processes in organizations and greater support for these processes rather than to administrative procedures and control.[8]

The findings of this book support much of the research on organizational creativity conducted since the sixties, as well as the approach developed by the members of the Association for Social Development.[9] Our work in many different organizations suggests that a mature institution facing a crisis of the "administrative" or differentiation phase needs to consciously enter a new cycle in its development, to opt for a new set of values, a different orientation toward work activity and simpler, decentralized structures. We believe this is as true for manufacturing companies as it is for service institutions, schools, and shops that have reached maturity.

Practically, this means that a mature institution needs to formulate a new set of simple, yet meaningful goals related to the essential products or services provided to clients. These goals need to be an integral part of the organization's past—its biography—to be authentic and to have the capacity of motivating both clients and coworkers or employees. What are a school's central educational goals and its educational philosophy, and how do they relate to the needs of both parents and students? What is a group of architects or a law firm really seeking to offer a client? Is a store or a company actually offering a set of quality products? It does not do to *say* quality or service to customers is

8. *Excellence*, 89–306.
9. See *The Phases of Organisation Development*, occasional paper, NPI Institute for Organisation Development, Zeist, Holland.

number one if it has never been so and there is no intention of making it a reality. Implied in this effort to reformulate goals or purposes is the recognition that people need to be able to find meaning in their work and their lives. An organizational culture that responds to this need in an honest way gains the commitment of its people and a direction and purpose for itself.

In the differentiation phase the basic aims of a school, a hospital, or a company tended to get lost over time as technical, administrative, and financial concerns became paramount. The focus of attention had quite properly shifted inward to make sure that things were functioning rationally. But the price of this inward focus is a loss of connection to clients and a dimming of the vision that made the initiative what it is. As in the beginning of the differentiation phase, an entry into full and conscious maturity, into the integration phase of the organization's life cycle, requires renewed attention to the initiative's central tasks and goals.

Implied in this reformulation of goals is waking up to the "sleeping partners" of the initiative, the customers and clients. The principle of association, of dialogue, needs to be adopted so that the initiative really knows the needs and preferences of those it seeks to serve. A school needs an active parent council and student council so that teachers, parents, students, and the community can have a frank discussion of needs and possibilities. A clinic or therapeutic center requires a patient group, and a farm or food store, a consumer circle. Only by taking such steps can the mature initiative avoid the one-sidedness of deciding by itself what an outside group needs, and keep its goals, products, and services in touch with changing people and a changing culture.

A second important aspect of the integration phase is the further development of the values and criteria that go into the organization's decision-making process. In the pioneer phase, customer satisfaction and survival were paramount while the economic base of the initiative was being built. In the next phase of development, administrative and technical criteria played an even greater role, so that the implementation of new information systems or production systems to increase efficiency were often more important than their impact on people. In the integration phase, technical, financial, and social or human criteria need to be consciously balanced. If one looks at an initiative as containing these three subsystems, then a decision in one area has implications for the others:

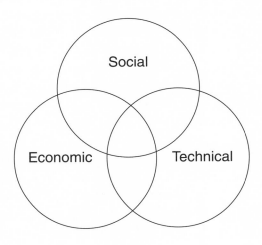

A new technical system will affect social relationships and financial outcomes. A new product line requires investment, training, shifts in work patterns, and new equipment. Any important decision needs to consider the consequences in these three areas and to include those measures or activities that will assure an integrated approach. Most important, the human impact of change needs to be considered and human needs taken more consciously into account in the integration phase.

A third area is related to this latter point—namely, a conscious understanding of the human being as the essential ingredient in any successful initiative. Most organizations going through the differentiation phase divide the work process in such a way that some people are involved in planning and delegating work (managers), others are involved in doing it (workers), and still others in controlling it and checking it (quality control). This division of work is, of course, most visible in large product organizations making cars, refrigerators, or tubular steel. However, it is also a tendency in law firms, doctors' offices, hospitals, and other initiatives where senior members plan work, less senior people do it, and others check and control. This simple division of labor is important, yet it has the consequence of using the soul capacities of people in a one-sided way. Who has not laughed or cried at the architect who has designed an office that is uninhabitable or a house that cannot be built because the designer did not understand either offices or building materials? Equally, we have all experienced a person doing a specific job and following instructions but not being able to carry them out properly because he did not really understand how they related to a customer's need. In the first case, the architect is using the ability to think in order to design; in the second a person is using his will to do.

Human beings, however, have three soul capacities: to think and plan, to will and do, and to feel and be responsible. The modern division of labor and the related high levels of specialization foster a one-sided development of these soul faculties. This tendency is particularly pronounced in the differentiation phase of an initiative. In the integration phase the three soul capacities again need to be more consciously taken into account in building semi-autonomous work or project teams that over time acquire the ability of planning, executing, and controlling their own work within general guidelines. The creation of such groups or teams requires delegation, open sharing of goals and other information, and often time and training. But without steps in this direction, people will use their ingenuity to circumvent time or quality systems, their feelings to "rip off" the organization, and their will to build model boats at home. A culture of excellence, of commitment, means not only creating an organization with worthwhile goals, but also one in which people have an opportunity of using their innate faculties for the benefit of the whole. A recognition of the full potential of human creativity also involves a commitment to professional development activities, flexibility in work hours and scheduling, and the fostering of individual initiative.

Self-administered initiatives in the cultural or service sphere may feel that these needs do not apply to them. But here too differentiation inevitably leads to the hiring of administrators, bookkeepers, secretaries, maintenance people, cooks and others. Teachers also should have an insight into the bookkeeping and the supply ordering system. The same people doing the same jobs for too many years fosters one-sidedness. The question then emerges, how can people be helped to both broaden their insights and balance the use of their capacities?

A key element for initiatives seeking to overcome the limitations of the differentiation phase is for individuals and teams to develop a new awareness of the central rhythms and work processes of the initiative, and structuring activities to facilitate these processes. In the differentiation phase the organization was understood and viewed more from a functional and hierarchical point of view. This perspective is a vertical consciousness leading to organization charts that look like Christmas trees with packages dangling from the boughs. In the integration phase a horizontal consciousness is needed. Simply put, an initiative needs a purpose, a set of questions it is responding to; it requires know-how and information to respond to this need; it organizes work activities to respond to the customer's or client's wants, and it does so by using financial, human, and technical resources. A school responds to the educational needs of children through a curriculum and philosophy of education, by guiding a sequence of educational activities from kindergarten through a number of grades, and using a building and teachers to carry out the educational process. Visualizing these activities leads to the following picture:

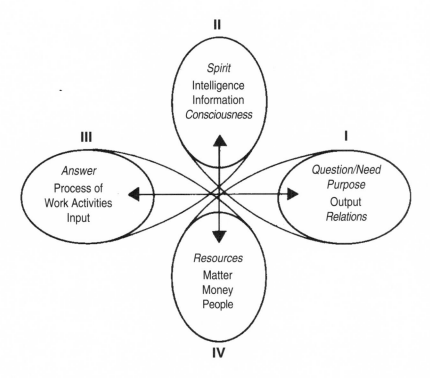

The qualities indicated in this picture can be translated into specific questions for mature organizations.

A Culture of Consciousness:
Questions for the Integration Phase

NEEDS, MISSION, PURPOSE —I

- What needs are you responding to? How are they articulated and by whom?
- Do you have regular means of dialogue with your customers or clients?
- How do you articulate your mission and purpose?
- Is this mission and purpose worthy of you and does it meet true human needs?

VISION, VALUES, AND POLICIES— II

- What is your central vision for the organization?
- What values are you pursuing in your organization?
- How are the vision and values articulated externally and internally?
- How are the values embodied in policies and relationships?
- How do you measure the success of the organization?
- Are the values such that they contribute to human creativity and to the responsible use of resources?

PROCESS AND ACTIVITY —III

- What are the central work processes of the organization?
- How are they presently organized?
- What is the rhythm and pattern of these activities?
- How can they be reorganized to enhance clarity and rhythm and the involvement and creativity of everyone?

RESOURCE— IV

- What are the resources, financial, material, and human that are required for the central work or service activities?
- What blocks presently exist in the effective use of resources?
- How can organization forms be changed so that these resources are more effectively used?
- How can your resources be shared easily with other organizations?

Asking such questions means bringing the dialogue with the spirit, with mission and purpose to consciousness; fostering and strengthening the dialogue with people, with customers, suppliers, and coworkers; and bringing more awareness to the dialogue with the earth, with finance, machinery, and work processes. As the institution moves from pioneer through differentiation into maturity ever more attention needs to be given to these dialogues so that the organization remains creative and does not resort to only finding meaning through market share, financial return, or enrollment figures. Ongoing renewal of this kind implies a real commitment to reviewing and learning from successes and failures and to monitoring the health of the whole organization. This is one of the central challenges of organizational leadership.[10]

The sequence of responding to needs by putting human ingenuity and resources to work is, of course, present from the time the initiative begins, but it is hidden. The trick in the integration phase is to see the organization as a process organism and to restructure it to enhance the central processes. If you think of a company from the viewpoint of the production process—inventory control, production teams, quality teams, shipping and delivery—you divide work vertically, usually blocking communication between segments while coordination takes place at higher management levels. The same is true of a clinic or even a self-administered school with many committees carrying out discrete functional tasks and referring to a central decision-making body for coordination. In the case of the company, a review of the central work process might lead to a production team having responsibility for purchasing, inventory control, quality control and shipping, as well as production. Certainly modern information systems now make it possible to contemplate such steps. The limitations are that management levels

---

10. See Max DePree, *Leadership Is an Art* (Dell, 1989), in particular pp. 11–22 and 53–62 on the important attributes and challenges of leadership.

would decrease and that information would need to be shared more fully. In addition, production teams would be required to accept increased responsibility. Quality circles and job enrichment experiments, have, however, indicated that such steps are not only possible but can lead to increased efficiency and greater worker satisfaction.

In self-administered schools, shops, or clinics, steps in this direction are also possible—perhaps by putting the functions of publicity, external relations, enrollment, and fund-raising into one committee, and generally simplifying the organization's structure in line with central work processes.

As part of the new process consciousness, a new awareness of the time rhythms affecting the initiative are important. What are the sales and production cycles? What are the weekly, monthly, and annual rhythms in the classroom? What is the appropriate time sequence for the budgeting and financial review process? What are the human requirements for rejuvenation and professional development?

By paying attention to this dimension of the organization, one is beginning to consciously build the habit life of the institution. It was always there, but in the differentiation phase the qualities of leadership, of administration were central so that a kind of soul differentiation took place in the organism. In the pioneer phase, on the other hand, the initial identity and the first aspects of the physical form, of buildings and facilities, were the focus of awareness.

The consequence of a new integrated process consciousness is also the creation of simpler, decentralized and flatter structures on a human scale. Limited administration and "lean" are current American phrases used to describe these qualities of the integration phase.

When an organization has moved toward integration, its ability to respond to its environment is enhanced, its internal functioning is more streamlined, and people can have a renewed sense of pride in their work. One can say it has achieved full maturity and a collective wisdom that also allows it to help other initiatives and to serve the wider needs of its community.

In summary, the qualities of the integration phase include:

1. Renewing central aims and the organization's values and culture to provide meaning. In practice this means an ongoing commitment to quality of service and/or product.
2. Creating the organs for an association—a conscious dialogue with customers, clients, suppliers, and the community in which the initiative is active.
3. A leadership and decision-making style that takes human needs into account, explicitly balancing financial, technical, and social criteria. Consciousness not limited to rational analysis.
4. An enhanced understanding of human beings and the creation of work processes and structures that take this new understanding of human capacities into account.
5. Creating a process organization in which structures reflect the requirements of central work processes rather than administrative control mechanisms. Paying attention to and enhancing the rhythmic quality of the initiative's life.
6. Building self-directed teams and smaller, decentralized and flatter organizational forms.
7. Process, horizontal thinking, rather than vertical and hierarchical thinking.

These qualities do not add up to an organizational blueprint. Rather, they suggest a type of awareness, a way of looking at and understanding organizations and people from a less analytical, but deeper, more whole and conscious perspective. This perspective and the resulting direction are being explored by many initiatives today, for we all face the question of what new organizational forms are appropriate for the highly individualized consciousness that we have in Western societies.

A Conscious Ending?

If the pioneer stage can be likened to childhood, the differentiation phase to early and middle adulthood, and the integration phase to full maturity and old age, what can be said about the death of an initiative? A convenient response is to say organizations die when they fail and are no longer needed. However, I feel that many institutions have not only become old, but also sclerotic, disposing of vast resources but no longer really serving human needs. What would happen to cultural, social, and economic creativity if institutions over one hundred years old turned over their resources to new groups wishing to respond to similar needs in new ways? What a peaceful ongoing creative revolution society would experience. To do so would require institutions to contemplate a conscious death process in order to allow a new resurrection. It is an intriguing thought, if not a present reality.

The Image of Development

What has been presented is a sketch of developmental patterns in organizations. Frequently I am asked, can't a stage be missed? The answer is no if organizations have a true life cycle moving from simple to more complex, from one central organizing principle to another. This means that true development is a discontinuous, irreversible process in time, moving from a stage of growth through differentiation to a higher stage of integration and passing through states of crisis that offer the impetus for development. This pattern is, I believe, true for all living forms, for the human being, and for organizations.

However, it is possible for initiatives to move more or less rapidly through these phases. A school that starts with six grades and a kindergarten will face questions of differentiation sooner than one that starts with one grade and adds a new grade each year. A company that has twenty employees the first year and four hundred the second will also face developmental issues more rapidly than one that grows more slowly. Furthermore, it is quite common for large organizations to have different divisions at different stages of development. A new product division may be in the pioneer stage, the mother company may be going through the crisis of differentiation, while an older division may already have started working with the principles of integration.

The described image of an initiative's development over time is incomplete. Like all ideal-type descriptions it cannot do justice to the rich texture of organizational life, nor to the uniqueness of each initiative.[11] Its purpose is rather to describe a landscape of possibilities, to indicate paths to be pursued and pitfalls to be avoided so that we may become more conscious and responsible co-creators on earth.

---

11. See Robert Chin, "The Utility of Systems Models and Developmental Models for Practitioners," in Bennis, Benne and Chin, *The Planning of Change* (NY: Holt, Rinehart and Winston, 1962), 201–215.

11

Building the Organization

3

Starting Initiatives

TŸNO VOORS

> Every person is a special kind of artist and every activity is
> a special art. An artist creates out of the materials of the
> moment, never again to be duplicated. This is ... true of
> us all, whatever our work, that we are artists so long as we
> are alive to the concreteness of the moment and do not
> use it for some other purpose.
>
> *M.C. Richards*

How can we foster the development of initiatives? How can
new enterprises such as community projects, schools, farms,
and businesses be well founded? How can we work together as
equals, sharing our responsibilities, encouraging each other
in our development, and offering a high quality product or
service?

These are questions many people ask. They are searching
and experimenting to find ways to take and sustain new initiatives that make a contribution to social renewal.

Many projects begin with great enthusiasm, good intentions,
useful ideas, capable people, and the necessary resources. But
many of these initiatives never really start, or disappear after a
short period. Other initiatives evolve, become visible, active and
successful, but soon are entangled in all kinds of difficulties
and conflicts.

Undertaking an initiative with others means working long
hours, many meetings, having a small income, taking great
risks, tiredness, lack of rhythm, and the feeling of never being
able to realize the ideal. It also means sharing responsibility and

possibilities to experiment and learn. And sometimes it means realizing ideals and sharing great successes.

In all my contacts with new initiatives over the last ten years I have been confronted time and again with the question: How can we make our initiative *work*? In reviewing their history, I often noticed that some aspects were neglected and others over-emphasized. The key for a more systematic approach and review of initiatives was finally provided when Ronnie Lessem, while working with URBED, introduced me to the concept of "from *Vision to Action*" developed by Kevin Kingsland.[1] This concept helped me realize that every initiative needs to nurture *seven basic aspects*. These are:

- Developing vision—recognizing the motive
- Answering a need
- Formulating direction
- Commitment of people
- Working together
- Managing processes and time
- Finding facilities and resources.

When starting, all initiatives go through a process of birth involving these seven basic needs.

There is an idea and a need is seen. Brochures are made indicating the direction. A group of co-workers that is really committed to the work is formed, and the initiative can start only if it can find a building and finances and can organize its work. In this process, some aspects receive a lot of attention

---

1. URBED—Urban and Economic Development Ltd.—fosters among other activities the development of new business and community projects, 99 Southwark St., London SE1 O3F, England. Dr. R. Lessem, director of Business Development Programme of City University and author of *The Roots of Excellence* (London: Fontana) and *Enterprise Development* (London: Gower). Kevin Kingsland, Centre for Human Communication, 19 Pearsons Park, Hull, Humberside.

and are discussed and wrestled with at length, while others are only mentioned at the beginning but not recognized as important and so will have to be dealt with later on.

1. Developing Vision —Recognizing the Motive

Sometimes we meet a person who has lived for a long time with the idea of starting something—be it a workshop, a café, a business, a school, a new institute or agency. He or she has been carrying around the germ of the idea—it keeps coming back time and time again as a picture of what might be, like a dream. But circumstances somehow contrive to never let it happen.

Then all of a sudden he or she meets another person who has been waiting for the same thing to happen. Then they may meet another...and another...who has a friend who...! Maybe the only thing they have in common is the idea. They begin to share their dreams, talk to each other with great enthusiasm, become excited and start making all kinds of tentative plans. Sometimes they may get a little carried away—but never mind! It is as if inside each one of them something significant has been touched. This is something that wants to get out, to begin moving, to start.

Such a complementarity of dreams is the source of the vision—a picture, an image of that which lives in the will of each initiative taker. In every initiative there is a need to make this explicit, as clear as possible—and to share it. This articulation can be difficult to do, for the inner stirrings are not easy to put into words. If we wait awhile and listen hard, one of the initiative-takers may be able to make a start, to put his feelings into words, helping others who cannot formulate these feelings so exactly.

When you want to take an initiative with a group of people who equally share the responsibility for the whole, then it is of utmost importance to develop *a sense of the motives that live in the different initiative-takers*. People bring their life experiences, their values, their expectations to the initiative, and everyone's life brings different colors. In their first enthusiasm they tend to see only that they agree and do not notice their differences. But later when there is no time, when there is the pressure of work, the differences are felt and can be the source of conflicts.

So it is worthwhile at the start and regularly in later years to find time to sit together and to listen to each person's individual goals and to recognize and mold common goals. I sometimes ask: "If this were an enterprise where you could realize your ideals, your hopes, your expectations, what would be the most important thing to realize?" If you then listen to these highly individual stories, the whole group can get a feeling of what there is in common and what differences have to be accommodated.

Through questions to each other, people start to realize that working together in a group brings much more than just skills. Everyone brings something that lives deeply hidden within his or her soul. Deep in their hearts, all people are searching for their life path, to meet their destiny. And in the process of meeting and working with others, something of one's destiny can be realized, something that one cannot realize alone.

Interest in the individuality of the other and respect for what is different are the basic attitudes that must exist in a group of people if they want to create something together. Self-interest and the over-valuing of one's own vision will in the long run create tensions and conflicts. People in an initiative can regularly ask each other:

- What do *you* want to realize in this initiative? Why is that important to us? What ideals, hopes, expectations can be realized? What guiding principles do you want to realize?

- What changes would this bring to our lives? How does this step relate to the rest of my life?

And listening to the contribution one can ask:

- What do we have in common and what differences do we have to accommodate?

There is still another aspect to the recognition of the motive. When a group of people works together the individuals in the group can achieve something together that cannot be achieved by each person alone. Just as with human beings—an initiative has an identity, something that makes it unique. A hundred schools may follow the same curriculum, but none of them is the same. So we must ask ourselves, what makes one school different from the other? Is it the alchemy of the different people or is it something of the new identity that wants to find expression through people?

So people taking initiatives can ask themselves:

- What is the identity of our work?
- What is it that wants to live among us?
- What can we make possible together?

2. Answering a Need

Initiatives that want to respond to the social or economic questions of today cannot only spring from an inner urge to do something. They must also be directed toward what other people are asking. The aim of every organization is *to meet the needs of others;* to respond to the questions and demands of their customers, clients, pupils, parents.

But how do you find out what people want, expect, and need?

An interesting approach to this question has been developed by Forum 3, a youth center in Stuttgart, Germany. The center is in the heart of the city, where people meet every evening in a coffee house or come together in study or action groups; they do artistic activities, or discuss contemporary political, social, or economic questions. Twice a year, staff members of Forum 3 invite their "customers" to look behind the scene of the activities of Forum 3 and indicate what they appreciate.

"Customers" are asked what they expect, and what they would like offered as activities. The Forum staff listen and ask questions. Later they review and conclude that activities need to be changed, developed, or discontinued. In this way, the staff tries to keep and develop a living contact with the larger customer group. Once a year, the staff members of Forum 3 do something else in a similar direction. They ask themselves what important questions are living in them. Through this process, they try to recognize the signs of the times. As a result they are often able to anticipate and prepare themselves for the demands of two or three years later.

The key to finding out what is asked, demanded, or needed is to try to creep into the skin of customers. Members of the initiative group must be open to every suggestion—look at it, taste it, weigh it. As someone once said to me: "Every suggestion by someone is a starting point for further thinking about the chances and reality of our initiative." The danger with everything you want to offer is that you are too self-confident and believe you know what is the best. On the other hand, do not lose your sense of direction by following every hint, or doubting yourself at every critical note.

To know what is wanted, to meet the interest of customers, an initiative must become visible. Members of the group will have to go out and speak about the initiative and see how people respond. To get information they have to be alert and observe well; they have to listen. At the start they may speak with friends, visit similar initiatives in other places or countries, organize evenings, meet with local politicians, write articles, listen to the responses, and see if they can find support.

Supporters are very important for an initiative that wants to stand in the world. True supporters are invaluable with their concrete suggestions, their help with the work, their smaller or larger financial backing, their warmth and interest—especially in the early days. Very few initiatives have come to birth without the help and sacrifice of many invisible helpers. Supporters are the warmth body of an initiative; they are the "mother" of the initiative; they prepare the environment.

Experiences with initiatives that are looking for financial support have also shown that it is helpful to find a number of supporters and ask them for a personal loan, or to act as personal guarantors for a loan. (See chapter 5.)

It is essential to stay in touch with the customers, to know what they want in the later years of an organization. You can wait for parents to send their children to another school, or you can anticipate the changes that will prepare pupils for the challenges of the turn of the century. If every organization would ask itself every year if it were still responding to the needs of its customers, fewer would be in trouble.

Asking the following questions will help you identify the needs of the people served by the initiative:

- Are we listening, observing, asking our customers what they expect of us?
- What do people really express in their needs? How do we know that the initiative is wanted?
- What needs, expectations, do people express that could be incorporated in the initiative or even give it a change of emphasis?
- What opportunities and what restrictions lie in the situation one meets?

- Are people willing and able to pay a price for our services?
- What are the current questions facing us, and what response are we making?

Of course you can never be totally sure the needs have been met until your customers have bought the product, filled the school, or come to the adult education center.

3. Formulating Direction

At a certain moment the initiative has to become more specific. It is good to have a dream, a great vision, or a deep motive to contribute something that brings social renewal. But these are often very large gestures that will be realized only in the distant future. It is necessary to confront this vision with the needs, the possibilities, and the limitations that are there now.

Members of the initiative have to develop a picture of how the initiative will function in two or three years' time. The time has come to stop orientating themselves by asking others what they expect and listening to their suggestions. It is time to become concrete. An excellent instrument for building this awareness is to start writing a brochure or to prepare material for a fund-raising appeal. In doing so, you dive into the process of formulating and reformulating, and have to guard against becoming abstract. What is written has to interest people, has to make them stop for a moment, has to work on their imagination.

You need a lot of imagination here in order to develop a living picture of the future. You have to play not only with words, but also with forms, colors, so that gradually an image of the school, the business, the curative home, or the counseling service becomes visible.

A brochure has to express:

- The name of the initiative or the product.
- Artistic representations of a central aspect of the name or the activities of the initiative.
- A short description of the history, the motive, and the general aims.
- A description of what members want to have achieved in the next two or three years, that is, what activities will be developed.
- A description of the basic attitude, style, approach to customers, coworkers, finances, and organization.

Formulating the direction is a confronting, painful, and sometimes agonizing process. One or two people will write, but will the product express what lives in the others? Often things are expressed that have not been discussed at all, and the pressure builds to agree because the appeal must go out. Often the first cracks in the beautiful harmony of intentions will start to show.

This process of choosing and formulating the direction is a constant, reoccurring necessity. New developments take place; the initiative grows; new products, services, classes, courses are offered. In many initiatives the move to a new building is a milestone in the biography of the initiative. You have to build or renovate. And again, you have to formulate, to choose direction.

This work is not only meant to reveal to the public what members of the initiative see as the central aims, style, and activities of the organization, but also serves as a focal point for discussions between the coworkers. Everyone should ask him or herself if they share this living picture of the future.

EXERCISE
FORMULATING DIRECTION

Making a Poster or Advertisement

A good activity to work on in determining the common direction of the initiative is to spend an evening with coworkers, making a poster or an advertisement for a special event, or a title page for a course brochure, or an appeal leaflet.

1. Someone briefly describes the main aspect of the event or coming activity.

       . . . . . .

2. Every coworker makes a poster, advertisement, or title page using words, key sentences, pictures, logo, layout, colors.

       . . . . . .

3. Coworkers share their work and a discussion follows on which words, sentences, pictures, and colors would draw attention and interest to the event. One can also discuss whether the poster expresses the true nature of the initiative.

4. Commitment of People

The previously mentioned aspects of recognizing the motive, answering a need, and formulating direction, will bring the underlying values of the initiative into consciousness. This process of becoming conscious of what people share and want to bring to expression together is very important for people today. Many more people want to contribute concretely by sharing the responsibility instead of following the leader, the boss, the director. However, people can start to act intelligently in the sense of the whole only if the direction, the vision of the future gradually becomes explicit. So initiatives that want to further co-responsibility have to return to these stages time and again in order to rekindle the flame that fired them. This process is also necessary for new people who join the initiative later, to give them an opportunity to connect with the aims.

There is, however, a danger of talking too much, of trying to bring everything to consciousness, of waiting until everyone has said that they will support the initiative. Potential coworkers, but also supporters and volunteers get impatient and want to see something start to happen. You have to start moving— someone must be willing to give up his previous job; another must follow; real preparation for action has to start. You will often see that the initiative group changes significantly. People have to take a step, risk their jobs, their income, the well-being of their family, without the certainty of success and security. This uncertainty seems less of a problem in the nineties with many people out of work or shifting careers. But it still remains an enormous step in which you not only commit yourself but also the people who are dependent upon you.

I remember a group of people who had been meeting together to prepare an initiative for working with young people. They were people with very different backgrounds: a gardener, a printer, a management consultant, a social worker, a maintenance man, a lecturer, an artist. When the step to begin was taken there were only two who could commit themselves; the others moved to the periphery, became supporters and volunteers. After a year most of them had moved and were involved with other things. At the same time, other people came forward, offering their help. Sometimes it looks as if secret smoke signals have gone through the valleys and over the hills, because people from far and wide have heard about and want to join the initiative.

The process of starting confronts the initiative-takers with the recurring question: *"How do we find our real partners?"* People who want to join have all kinds of different motives; how do you find the criteria to choose among them? You are confronted here with one of the hardest questions of life. People's feet have brought them to this place. Are they passing by, are they asking for shelter, are they bringing the skills needed to offer quality, do they fit into the team? You cannot be sure in the first meeting but have to guard against hurried commitments. Especially when finding your colleagues you have to take time. I know of a school that is in great need of teachers. People come to fill the job, but when the personnel group of the school, and especially one person who is respected for her clear, deep, and mostly sound judgement, expresses reservations, then the person is not invited to join and the children do not have that subject. This example stands in strong contrast to the attitude of another school that invited people to join as teachers because the children needed a teacher. The result of that policy is that this school has too many colleagues who do not understand the basic direction of the school.

A way of approaching this question is to make it a policy to answer the following questions:

1. Do we see each other as *initiative* partners, carriers of the same aims and impulses, wanting to serve similar needs?

2. Are we willing to commit to each other, to respect each other in our differences, and to accept the consequences of each other's activities?
3. Do we have the capacities that are needed *to do the work* and do our capacities and skills complement each other?

The same questions can be expressed differently as was the case with a small company making natural medicines. They approach every vacancy filled from inside or outside by asking themselves the following questions:

Is the person:

- Willing and capable of doing the job?
- Willing and capable of working together with us?
- Committed to the aims and development of the company? Willing to accept the salary policy?

The last point was important because it emphasized the different character of the salary arrangement in this company.

These questions can never be answered with a straight yes or no. Answers will emerge in conversations and working together.

To find out if there is a group of individuals that is really willing to commit itself to the work, the following questions might be helpful:

- What risks are people willing and able to take?
- Is there enough patience, endurance, courage, and commitment in the group to succeed?
- Who are the carriers, who are the supporters, the volunteers?
- What personal investment of others (dependents) or resources of others are we risking with this step?

5. Working Together

Every group that has decided to work together to answer an identified need has to start to organize itself. Every small or large initiative has to nurture a whole network of relationships.

When we look more closely at these relationships we can distinguish among them by the degree of direct involvement in the enterprise.

First of all you have the group that consists of customers (for example, clients, patients, or parents), suppliers, banks, local and government institutions, and so on. The initiative can aim to develop a regular contact with groups of customers. It is becoming more and more important to connect with similar initiatives or enterprises in the region, thus forming an association or network as a source for professional exchange.[2] Many of these associations or networks exist among schools, curative homes, shops, and consultants. They often provide a platform for the exchange and development of ideas about new approaches, methods, and concepts. These associations or networks, in which every institution stays independent, work on the basis of recognized interdependence and trust, and the understanding is that by complementing and supporting every one, each group has more of a chance to become a mature organization.

A circle of relations closer to the initiative consists of the supporters, volunteers, guarantors, financial benefactors, accountants or bookkeepers, and of course the trustees or members of the board. These people often play a very important role during the early life of the initiative. Not so much because they have a formal position on the board, but because they strengthen the initiative with their expertise, guidance, extra donations, enthusiasm, or unlimited supply of helping hands. Their role can sometimes be influential, as was the case with a

---

2. John Naisbitt, *Megatrends*, (NY: Warner Books, 1984).

school where a group of parents made all the plans and organized all the finances for the development of the school and a move to a new building. In more established schools, one usually sees the reverse. The teachers decide everything and use the parents when it suits them.

The circle of real supporters is of vital importance for the life of every organization. It is the warmth body without which no institution can stay healthy in the long run. Their honesty, concern, wisdom, and respect can keep the coworkers awake, alert and open to new developments. The supporters provide the fresh air in which the initiative can breathe.

The closest circle of relationships that has to be nurtured is the group of coworkers. How do we work together? How do we make decisions? How do we organize the work responsibilities? How do we deal with salaries, ownership, and profit-sharing? These questions are born out of a longing to find new social forms that are challenging, that create the possibility of taking on new responsibilities, of learning to develop. These forms are not more efficient or easier; they do not create more harmonious relationships. They challenge, and demand of people a new social understanding, an attitude of interest and respect toward others, and the use of social skills. Especially when working together to build co-responsibility you meet each other and yourself more intensely. It is my experience that no new social forms succeed without the commitment of the coworkers to work on themselves. (See chapter 9.)

One often sees that when there are strong expectations and verbal acknowledgments to work together as equals, the reality may be very different. Then the initiative begins to struggle with crises, giving rise to all kinds of misunderstandings, bad feelings, heated arguments, and, ultimately, to conflict.

RELATIONSHIP MAP

Working together needs to take place on several levels within and around the organization. Coworkers, supporters, and clients are all involved in various dialogues. Association is based upon freely willed dialogue. It cannot be legislated, but is created out of the recognition that each independent unit can be strengthened in such a relationship.

Coworkers

How do we make decisions?   Ownership? Profit Sharing?, etc.

How do we deal with salaries?   Focus is on internal arrangements.

COWORKERS

SUPPORTERS

CLIENTS

Supporters

Become board members, formalizing the initial warmth and enthusiasm.

Forms arise—legal, administrative, financial, banking, capital.

Clients

Who are our clients?

How do we know their needs?

How can we evaluate our products and services against their needs? How can we foster a dialogue with them?

Society, community. Also other groups working in the same market, and other related groups. Formation of networks, associations, federations, movements.

In the realm of working together, questions to consider are:

- How do we relate to our customers, suppliers, connected initiatives, bank, government? What style and form do we want to develop?
- How will we relate to our supporters, volunteers, benefactors, trustees, members of the board? What is the best legal form for our initiative?
- How do we want to organize ourselves? Who decides about what, and how do we reach decisions? What will be our approach to salaries?
- How willing are we to work on ourselves?

6. Managing Processes and Time

Have you ever been involved in a whole-foods restaurant, or an organization of adult classes, a toymaking workshop, or a bakery? In these initiatives you will see many of the coworkers very actively involved during the day running the work processes. The guest in the restaurant wants a warm, well-prepared, well-served meal. What has to happen for that to take place is tremendous. How many ingredients are used in the meal, where do they come from, how did they arrive in the kitchen, how many people have been involved to make it possible so that you can have this meal? If you really try to imagine this you will discover that many, many activities are interconnected, that everything we buy in a shop, or eat in a restaurant is the end result of incredibly complicated work processes.

You could say that the work processes are the lifeblood of the initiative. A constant transformation, an alchemy takes place, in which raw materials, hands, machines, human creativity, communication, and time work together in such a way that the miracle happens time and again. In the history of the industrial revolution you can notice that much research went into simplifying work processes, giving to the machine those work processes that could be repeated. The result of this mechanization, however, was that workers had to follow the machines in repetitive, routine work.

Such rationalization is not usually the experience of people when they start their enterprise. What you mostly see is a great talent to improvise; a dependency on the experience of one or two people who seem to be in charge of everything; constant pressure to deliver on time; chronic overwork to make ends meet. As a result, you see a lot of life and activity, but limited rhythm. Often it looks to me as if the initiative is running out of breath; showing signs of hyperventilation. Many people in the initiatives suffer from the lack of rhythm, the feeling that nothing can be finished, the constant pressure.

So there is a great need to pay some attention to the running of the work processes so that they can provide a rhythm to the activity, and be run efficiently. For example, a farmer once told me that he was always having difficulties with the yogurt-making on the farm. So I asked him to write down what activities had to be done, in which order, to make the yogurt. I asked him: "Try to think through the process from the moment the milk leaves the cow to the moment the yogurt carton is sold." A week later he told me that by writing all these activities down he had already noticed that two or three things could be done better and faster. He gave this list to an artist who was interested in these processes with the question: "Can you make these processes visible so that the yogurt maker, the apprentices, and other helpers can look at it and know what has to be done next?"

Work processes need to be thought through with great care but also observed and regularly reviewed after the initiative has started. During the preparation one will realize that everything cannot be done at once and that it is necessary to set priorities. It is fantastic *to do* many things together and the better prepared people are, the more they are able to understand each other with half a word. But time *to review*, to take stock, to breathe, to keep people and the ship on course has to be set aside and planned.

Questions to nurture this aspect are:

- Which work processes are needed to do the work and how can they be organized in the most effective way?
- What are our priorities?
- How do we organize our work life? When do we meet? Who prepares what? Who coordinates all activities? Who is responsible for planning?

7. Finding Facilities and Resources

No initiative can start without a space (a room, house, building, workshop), furniture, tools, materials, and machines. Space can be bought or rented, furniture, tools and machines bought new or secondhand. All can be renovated, decorated, or cleaned with the help of volunteer work, but in the end one needs to find a sum of money to finance the beginning of the initiative.

It is often a long search to find the right space and every initiative goes through endless deliberations to decide if it can afford the space or not. If you decide that this is the place, you have to go out and find the money. Many things need to be prepared for the bank, foundations, or close relatives of the initiative-takers in order to come up with the necessary capital.

You have to describe the history, aims, and proposed activities of the initiative (as described above under Formulating Direction) as well as describing in detail the possibilities of the space, the costs of renovation, and the value of the building if you want to buy it. The same applies to furniture, materials, tools, machinery. You often need to add to the personnel costs to make it possible for some of the future coworkers to have a salary at the beginning.

EXERCISE

Observing Work Processes

When a group of people wants to look at the way they organize their work processes, it is helpful for each person to answer the following questions:

1a. Whose needs does your work directly serve? (This may be an external client, or someone in the same organization whose work is dependent on yours.)

   b. How direct is your relation to this person/people? How accurately and frequently are you able to check what they require of you?

2a. Who allocates tasks to you? To whom do you allocate tasks?

   b. How directly orientated are these tasks to the needs of your actual "client"?

3a. What patterns of communication, accountability, and control are you involved in?

   b. Where are these helpful in supporting and guiding your work, and where do you find them inadequate, obtrusive, or irrelevant?

4a. What resources (physical, financial, personal) are available for your use?

   b. Are these adequate, inadequate, or superfluous?

5a. How would you characterize the leadership style in your organization? e.g.,autocratic/democratic/bureaucratic/functional/individualistic.

   b. Do you feel this style maximizes the effectiveness of your work? If not, in which direction would it need to change?

   c. Do you experience enough scope for your own initiative and innovation?

6. (To be discussed with colleagues): What concrete steps could we take in any of these areas to enhance our effectiveness?

The initial budget of the initiative could be called the *investment budget*, in which you can even indicate the priorities and the times when these items must be financed.

In addition to the investment budget, every initiative must calculate the income and expenditure of the initiative in the first year and the expected growth over the next years, including the interest and repayment of capital. If you do these calculations with great care and realism, with the help of an accountant or someone who is running a similar enterprise, it will become visible how much loan capital the initiative can carry and how much must be raised in gifts or venture capital. With these figures you can go to an established bank. If already available in your country, you could go to a bank institution like Mercury Provident Society in England, Triodos in Holland, or the Rudolf Steiner Foundation in the United States, all of which specialize in helping new initiatives raise the proper finances.[3] Together with such a bank you can create a fund-raising plan and make use of the bank's experience with different forms of raising gifts, establishing a borrowing community, and finding personal guarantors.

If the initiative group has paid enough attention to the aspect described in this chapter, it will be well received by the bank and can expect to work creatively with the bank.

Another aspect of the material foundation of the initiative is the care and artistic quality of the environment you are creating for the work. It does not have to be brand new or very modern, but you can do a lot with the choice of color of the walls, flowers, cleaned and painted furniture. The space is the place where the coworkers will be every day for many hours; the place where you meet your customers, the school children, the guests, the students. It is the space where people breathe an atmosphere

---

3. Mercury Provident Society. A new banking institution aiming to bring consciousness and social responsibility in the realm of money (see chapter 5).

prepared with care, and the touch of artistic quality can be experienced as a breath of fresh air in an overly functional world.

When preparing the facilities and looking for (or finding) the finances, ask yourself the following questions:

- What kind of space, environment, and machinery do we need?
- What is our investment budget?
- What is our expected income and expenditure for the next two years?
- How much can we afford to borrow and how much must we raise in gifts?
- Who are the people, the institutions that could help us?
- What material do we have to prepare for the fund-raising?
- What quality of environment do we want to offer to our customers and coworkers?

All of the above-mentioned seven basic aspects play a part in every initiative, and in already existing organizations or enterprises. Some of the aspects will be taken up more consciously than others; some are the focus of attention at a particular time. All have their place and together they form a totality. The first three aspects belong together and with their light and quality can penetrate the more concrete and material aspects described in the last three aspects. In the middle stands the group of committed people, who are willing to take up the challenge, be creative, and use the initiative as a free space in which they can make a positive contribution to society and to the future.[4]

---

4. Also read the excellent book by Paul Hawken, *Growing a Business* (NY: Simon and Schuster, 1987).

STARTING AND NURTURING
SOCIAL INITIATIVES
Checklist of Questions

1 / RECOGNIZING THE VISION

AIM: *To develop a sense of the motives that live in the different initiative-takers.*

- What do we want to realize with this initiative?
- Why is this important to each of us?
- What hopes, ideals, expectations could be realized?
- What changes would this bring to your life?
- How does this step relate to the rest of your biography?

When listening to the contributions of other initiative-takers one can ask:

- What do we have in common and what differences do we have to accommodate?
- What is it that wants to live between us?
- What can we as an initiative-group make possible together? What can we not realize on our own?
- What is the identity of our work?
- What can we make possible together?

2 / ANSWERING A NEED

AIM: *To understand the needs of the customer.*

- Have we been and are we listening, observing, and asking our customers what they expect? How are we going about this?
- What do people really express as their needs? How do we know that the initiative is needed?
- What needs, expectations do people express that could be incorporated in the initiative or even give it a change of emphasis?
- What opportunities and what restrictions lie in the situation one meets?
- Are people willing and able to pay a price for our services?

And more general:
- What are trends, signals of the time and is the initiative a response to them?

3 / FORMULATING DIRECTION

AIM: *To develop a living picture of how the initiative will function in 2 or 3 years. Make a brochure to express:*
- The name of the initiative.
- Artistic representations of a central aspect of the name or the activities of the initiative.
- A short description of the history, the motive, the general aims, and main activities.

Try to further describe:
- What coworkers want to have achieved within the next 2 or 3 years, what activities will be developed.
- The basic style, the basic attitude of working within the initiative and in relation to customers, community, suppliers, financiers.

4 / COMMITMENT OF PEOPLE

AIM: *To find the network of people that will nurture and carry the initiative.*
- What criteria do you want to use to find your potential colleagues, supporters, or volunteers?
- What risks are people willing and able to take?
- Is there enough patience, endurance, courage, ambition in the group to succeed?
- Who will be the carriers, who are the supporters?
- What personal investments of others (dependents) or resources of others are we risking with this step?

5 / WORKING OGETHER

AIM: *To describe the way you are to organize the initiative.*
- How do we want to organize ourselves?
- How will we communicate, when will we meet, who decides about what?

- How will we relate to our supporters, volunteers, benefactors, trustees, members of the board?
- What is the best legal form for our initiative?
- How will we approach the question of salaries?
- How willing are we to work on ourselves?

6 / MANAGING PROCESSES AND TIME

AIM: *To observe and describe the work processes that make the initiative fulfill its task.*

- Which work processes are needed to do the work and how can they be organized in the most effective way?
- What are our priorities?
- How will we organize our work life? What different functions have to be taken care of? Who will coordinate the activities?
- Who is responsible for the planning?

7 / FINDING FACILITIES AND RESOURCES

AIM: *To build a realistic picture of the facilities and financial needs of the initiative.*

- What kind of space, environment, machinery do we need?
- What quality of environment do we want to offer to our customers and coworkers?
- What is our investment budget?
- What is our expected income and expenditure for the next two years?
- How much can we afford to borrow and how much can we raise in gifts?
- Who are the people, the institutions that could help us?
- What material do we have to prepare for fund-raising?

WHY DO INITIATIVES FAIL?

Problem Diagnosis Using The "Seven Steps"

1 / Recognizing the Motive

- Loss of enthusiasm after "honeymoon" period.
- Loss of energy when routine sets in or obstacles are encountered.
- Loss of direction of long-term aims, constantly compromised to adapt to circumstances.
- Unrealistic, overambitious schemes.

2 / Answering a Need

- Losing touch with changing requirements.
- Preoccupation with internal management reduces client/customer orientation.
- Failure to maintain effective promotion and research.

3 / Formulating Direction

- Falling quality.
- Obsolescence.
- Overtaken by competitors.
- Price no longer attractive.

4 / Commitment of People

- Skills not adequate.
- Effort too low or misdirected.
- Avoidance of risk—missed opportunities.

5 / Organization of Relationships—Working Together

- Inappropriate legal structure.
- Failure to make clear agreements about ownership, decision-making, profit sharing.
- Inappropriate leadership style/lack of leadership.
- Bureaucracy—reduced motivation of staff.
- Poor communication, conflicts.

6. / Managing Processes and Time

- Lack of effective work planning and supervision.
- Inefficiencies due to:
- Poor equipment/facilities,
- Purchasing policy,
- Production methods,
- Administration procedures.
- Lack of feedback information re costs/benefits.
- Inflexibility of processes in response to changed needs.

7 / Finding Resources and Facilities

- Undercapitalization, inadequate financial control,
- Waste,
- Shortages of key supplies,
- Overextension.

4

Getting Going

The Growing Pains and Childhood Diseases of Initiatives

TŸNO VOORS

The impeded stream is the one that sings.

Wendell Berry

Many legends describe the story of a young person going out into the world. There are many trials and temptations. There are obstacles to overcome, and many tasks to carry out in order to successfully complete the journey.

This also happens with new initiatives. Initiatives often go through a long period of trial and error before they establish themselves in the world. Starting an initiative is meeting a challenge, is taking a step into the unknown. In changing something in an existing organization, or in starting something new, you meet resistance. No initiative can come to full maturity without going through a process of learning and development. Trials and temptations are outwardly experienced as forces that want to destroy the initiative, as forms of illness. Inwardly they can be seen as forces of resistance which, if met and learned from, can create a stronger group of people, more able to meet the tasks at hand.

This chapter describes some of the trials and temptations that new initiatives face. They are drawn from the experience of the Triodos Bank in Holland. Alexander Bos, one of the members of the Triodos group, was able to recognize and describe a number of these characteristic struggles.[1] One useful perspective from which to view the challenges that face new initiatives is that of childhood illnesses. These are to some degree inevitable and seem to strengthen the child, allowing its individuality to emerge more clearly. Yet it is important to know something of these illnesses in order to be able to treat them. The same can be said of the challenges or illnesses of new initiatives. They cannot be altogether avoided; they serve to strengthen the initiative if overcome, but it is important to know something about them before starting off on the journey.

A "Silver Spoon"

Everyone who has seen an initiative almost die for lack of funds knows the seductive thought, "If only we could get a legacy of twenty-thousand from somewhere, our problems would be solved." One starts to think about Uncle George or Aunt Nellie—they have given so generously to that other initiative. Isn't it our turn now? Another wished- for "uncle" can be the Government, or a large foundation.

In fact, one large donation or the total subsidizing of an initiative can be one of the worst things that can happen. It looks as if the time is now, the ideals can become a reality, talking is over, we can start. I can still remember how impressed I was when I first entered a new shop, a nicely decorated former theater. You could walk from one section to another, and buy your vegetables, groceries, books, toys, pure woolen clothes. You could wander from one place to another and marvel at the quality and the taste. Prices were stiff, but things were very well presented. On the "stage" was a coffee corner and an exhibition. Marvelous!

---

1. The Triodos Bank is a "sister" bank to the British Mercury Provident Society Ltd., which is described in chapter 6.

Alexander Bos's ideas are also described in Martin Large, *Social Ecology*, 135–137.

Within a year there were serious financial problems; supply and stock had to be drastically limited. The space looked empty, too big. The "spoon," the beautiful theater space, had proved to be too good and too expensive.

Similar things happen when someone offers an initiative a beautiful building for a school, or a medical center, when it is just starting. The same can happen when one receives a substantial sum of money to start a series of publications on a very important subject. However, after two issues the money is gone. Where are the buyers to finance the next?

What is happening, or not happening, in this situation? One has seemingly received an answer to the question of whether the initiative is really needed. An initial donation, gift, subsidy, or legacy has made a big step possible. But clients, patients, students, need to guarantee an initiative's existence. Such support can only be generated over time. If customers are not coming to the shop after an initial show of interest; if people do not become regular readers of the magazine; if only a few children come to the school; then one has to ask oneself: "Was the initiative really needed?"

We saw in the previous chapter how important it is to answer a need, to find recognition and support for the initiative in its immediate environment. When there is no large gift, no fine building, no silver spoon, then the initiative-takers have to engage in the long and often tiresome tasks of finding many gifts, and a variety of supporters. That means meeting people, talking about the initiative, to create enthusiasm and support.

Such effort creates new realities. The initiative group is forced to go beyond the small and immediate circle of friends. This outreach strengthens its sense of purpose, clarifies its aim, and helps it to develop a real dialogue with the environment. To be forced to articulate the essential aspects of the initiative can also help to make visible the fact that different members of the group have quite different pictures of the initiative. You can discover these differences when you meet with people and listen to how others are speaking about plans for the future. Sometimes you can have the feeling: "Is he really talking about the same thing?" To experience such divergent perspectives can often help in facing differences at an early stage, thereby avoiding difficult conflicts later.

To interest many people in giving small donations to the initiative creates much more than the sum total of these small gifts. Small gifts often come from a warm heart. Large subsidies, legacies, or grants can be quite cold. One does not have to refuse them, but they may not create the mantle of warmth, so important for a small infant.

Grand Propaganda

Over many years an individual had lived with a pet project. The idea had grown and grown, almost to the exclusion of everything else. This idea simply had to become reality. He thought of a community and adult education center. Many people were waiting for this initiative to be realized. The ideal building and grounds were found and brochures were sent all over Europe. Many people were talking about this grand idea and were inspired. It touched something they had been waiting for. Some came, selling their property to help to finance this new venture. Others came because they had heard about it and expected that they could start a new life. There were large meetings to discuss the future and all the work that had to be done. People worked on the buildings, and moved in. But people need to be fed, to be paid, and to live. Gradually questions appeared:

- Were all these people really needed to prepare for the task?
- Who was responsible for feeding everyone?
- Who should handle the money?
- Where were the resources to be found to help the initiative through the preparation period?

- Was everyone deciding everything together? Or did all depend on the initiator, the pioneer, the owner, and the financier?

Nothing dramatic happened, but gradually people left. Money that was promised did not materialize. Money that had been borrowed for a short period was asked to be returned. Feelings of deception, defeat, disappointment, and anger arose. Mutual accusations abounded. The window that people had been looking through into a potentially beautiful garden had shattered.

In this example a number of difficulties can be recognized. One of them is that a person or a group of people falls in love with his/her own idea. They cannot think of anything else, and the feeling grows stronger every day that they are chosen to bring this idea into reality. The group says: "It is very clear that the world is waiting for us, waiting for this idea. We want to bring good to the world with our idea." Ideas often have a strong influence on people, even to the degree that they can possess individuals. It is possible to live so strongly with an idea that one loses the ability to observe what reality needs to be created, and what is actually called for. Perception is distorted, and a dialogue with the environment is missing.

It is like Narcissus, a figure from mythology. He discovers his image in a lake and falls in love with it. This also happens with ideas and ideals. Self-love creeps into them and observation gets obscured. Difficulties are multiplied. When other people draw attention to some of the consequences, they are ignored, or told that they do not understand the true nature of the initiative. Questions are regarded as hostile and supporters who wish to help realistically are labelled "adversaries." Symptoms of fanaticism, paranoia, and martyrdom begin to appear.

The above example also shows us another childhood disease. We spoke about the need for every initiative to find recognition and support in its environment. Some people, however, have the gift to speak and communicate in such a way that potential coworkers, supporters, givers are immediately taken in by the beauty of the possibilities. Such individuals can awaken support in people and affect their independent judgement. However, the golden tongue—good propaganda—often leaves a bad taste, a sense of being cheated if the initiative was not grounded and the information given not true.

The beautiful idea and the gift of persuasion can serve to hinder a genuine dialogue with people about what is really needed and what they want to do and to support; while both of these qualities are needed, in excess they work as a drug that blocks hard work and the necessary realism.

Do It All Yourself

An initiative can experience a quite different illness when people think they have to do it all by themselves, with no external help. Being independent, running one's own show, being self-supporting and autonomous becomes the motto. You hear the sentiment expressed: "An initiative that has some self-respect should be able to carry itself from the start."

Such an orientation means that the initiative group goes to a bank to borrow the necessary amount for capital and start-up cost. At best it tries to get a lower interest rate. As a consequence it often has to start paying interest before the initiative has properly been launched, and a proportion of the loan will have to be repaid after half a year or a year. The question arises whether financing of this kind is appropriate in the early stages. It may be that a combination of gifts and loans is better, depending on what kind of initiative it is.

Through excessive self-reliance and early over-borrowing a number of initiatives that Triodos in Holland worked with ran into difficulties. One example was a group of people who wanted to start a whole-food restaurant. The group had imagined that the restaurant would pay for itself within the first year. The calculation worked out on paper: "So many meals and so many drinks for such a price makes such and such an income."

Reality, of course, was different. It takes at least a year before a restaurant has found its place in the neighborhood. It takes a while before customers have found their way to the restaurant; the quality of food, meetings, types of people, and atmosphere all need to be experienced. Actual costs are normally higher than expected, and income less than hoped for.

Another example was a bookstore in the United States that started with a large bank loan at high interest. While it was reasonably successful it struggled with this loan for its entire existence—thereby not having the possibility of expanding into the cultural activities that the founder wanted.

It lies in the nature of things that new initiatives need the help of free gifts to make a good start. Gifts are also a sign that the initiative is really wanted and supported. Because they are free, one does not begin with a heavy obligation to be financially successful from the start. New developments need to spread their wings. Gifts make this possible. Later on, loans for a new building or for expansion are right because the initiative is established and financially stable.

The Ideal Model

Some initiatives are hindered in their development because they start with a fully worked out structure and form. A foundation is created with buildings, investment structures, request forms all worked out. A limited liability company is incorporated, complete with directors and an advisory board, a totally worked out organization chart with functional descriptions, scheduled meetings, and procedures. Even income and expenditure accounts are projected for the next three years, but all before any actual activity has started.

What is really happening here? People are creating legal, organizational, and social form without content. Much thought and deliberation have gone into this organization structure. Coworkers, board members, even customers are somehow expected to feel at ease in these neatly designed forms. The reality is often the reverse. Coworkers experience a dogmatism that hinders free initiative and organic development. It is as if these structure-creators have given up on life. True observation of life shows us that life creates its own forms. The stream will create its own bed. Form and movement must enter into a conversation. Some form, of course, is needed in the early stages of an initiative, but the right form for a particular initiative has to evolve gradually out of the work—out of the flow of activities.

Over-organization can appear because of the desire for security or from ideological models. A Cooperative model, a Participative Community model, an Egalitarian model, and the Waldorf School model are a few examples. Ideals and values are of course important and should be reflected in structures, but an early overemphasis on values and ideals runs the risk that dogma becomes both authority and reality, and people and the initiative just the means to realize them.

The Absent Initiative-Taker

A similar difficulty can be experienced when someone has a brilliant idea, but others have to execute it. Here one can see the temptation of expecting others to realize your dream, to nurture your initiative.

These types of issues were evident in the following situation. Someone had observed the need to create a center for treating drug addicts that would use a therapeutic approach involving medical, artistic, and biographical help. Yet there was a need for staff. A group was found after an initial struggle. This group started the project and realized something of the initial idea, but the person whose idea it was could not just follow it from a distance and help with counsel when asked. Instead, he interfered every time the initiative went in a direction that did not coincide with his expectations. Tension, conflict, and ultimately a break in the relationship were the inevitable result.

The Negative Umbrella

Over the last few decades, more and more parents have questioned the quality of public or state education. They were not happy with the education but did not want to, or could not afford to, send their children to private schools. However, they wanted an "alternative" school. Perhaps they had heard that elsewhere groups of parents were founding Waldorf or Montessori schools, and they decided to do something similar.

They would often start by finding a house or empty school, cleaning it, and decorating it. Small chairs and desks were acquired from a school that had just closed. A foundation was formed with a board of strong enthusiastic parents, and with lots of effort a teacher was found to take the first class. Quite a number of parents had been waiting for this and decided to send their children. The school started, friends and the community were invited for an Open Day, and everyone was excited and happy.

However, even during the start-up period in such a school, certain misunderstandings and tensions can become evident, but the enthusiasm to create an alternative form of education initially prevails. Gradually it dawns on the initiative-takers that they have found each other *through the rejection of the old,* but their views of the alternative, of the positive and new, are very different. Everyone has their own concept of the alternative, often related to their own values of education and childrearing. Under the Negative Umbrella of the alternative school

Too Rapid Growth

There is also a danger in too much success. A new store starts, and all of a sudden the orders come in so quickly that a more orderly growth process becomes impossible. A store in Montreal selling cotton mattresses started selling direct to customers in street markets and through direct orders. It soon began to grow so that a manufacturing and retail operation was required. The initiators felt as if they were chasing cotton down a hillside but hardly gaining on it. Such experiences are quite common and can lead to stress, confusion, and a feeling of being over-whelmed. Like the demands of routine, the demands of excessive growth can obscure original intentions and lead the initiative in unwanted directions. The pressures of hiring, training, bookkeeping, supervising, ordering, and selling can become too much. Here too a pause, a period of reflection, is required and a setting of priorities so that the relative chaos can still reflect something of the earlier intentions.

Conclusion

We have discussed some of the typical trials that new initiatives face in the early phases of their development. The list of trials, of childhood diseases, is of course not complete. You may, out of your experience, describe others such as the Know-It-All Pioneer, the Perfect but Unwanted Product, or the Overstaffed and Overoptimistic School. What is important is to recognize that these trials or illnesses are to a greater or lesser extent inevitable and that if they are met and worked on they lead to a greater health for the initiative, and more understanding and self-knowledge for the initiative takers. If the attitude of learning from successes and failures, of gaining new insights from experience prevails, then the initiative will live, and the infant has a good chance of growing to maturity.

THE DRAGONS

A way of visualizing the struggles of initiatives is to see them as an army of dragons trying to devour the initiative. When these dragons are conquered, the initiative becomes stronger and socially fruitful.

1 / The Disintegration Dragon

Many initiative-takers have found each other through rejection of the old, but their views of the alternative, of the positive, are often different. Differences in motives, basic orientations, expectations of the members of the initiative can very soon lead to disintegration.

2 / The Sect Dragon

An initiative must always guard itself against the temptation of blindly believing in having found the pure motive. If this happens it withdraws in sect-like self-sufficiency.

3 / The Silver Spoon or Subsidy Dragon

The large gift at the start can prevent the initiative from working for its recognition in the environment. Lack of money might mean that the initiative is not ready to be born yet, or has no reason to exist at all.

4/ The Autonomy or "Go-It-Alone" Dragon

Some people think they can do it all by themselves, with no external help. Being independent, being self-supporting and autonomous, becomes the motto. "An initiative that has some self-respect should be able to carry itself from the start." But actual costs are normally higher than expected and income less than hoped for.

5 / The Adapting Dragon

"Let's be tolerant—all the different ways of looking at education/therapy, etc., have their validity!" This is, however, not always practical, because the inevitable compromise leads either to a colorless experiment or to the withdrawal of everyone's support.

6 / The Ideal Model Dragon

Starting with a fully worked-out structure of a "cooperative model," an "egalitarian model," or a "free school model," etc., will hinder free initiative and organic development.

7 / The Absent Initiative-Taker Dragon
or Delegation Dragon

Someone has a brilliant idea, but others have to execute it. It is the temptation to expect others to realize one's dream, especially when a group takes the initiative, but the initiator continues giving instructions to the executors.

8 / The Solo Dragon

The pioneer can be so strong that others are prevented from feeling co-responsibility. The danger is that the initiative becomes one-sided and dependent on the pioneer alone, with a nice bunch of followers. The initiative can very rapidly disappear with the father or mother figure.

9 / The Hurry Dragon

Just like babies, initiatives need time for maturing, for gestation. The hurry dragon whispers to us that this is the hour to act, to start, and not to sit back and contemplate. In this way premature births come about that will suffer an early death.

10 / The Expansion Dragon or Too-Rapid Growth Dragon

Some initiatives seem so relevant that they are threatened by expansive growth. But growth asks for new coworkers with adequate capabilities and for rapid organizational changes, otherwise the initiative grows itself to pieces.

11 / The Dilettante Dragon

Every initiative needs capable people, willing to learn and develop themselves. The dilettante dragon whispers to us continuously in the ear that we can stay as the one we are already. The result is a "Nice" initiative with a bunch of well-meaning amateurs.

12 / The Routine Dragon

Every initiative is in conflict with daily reality. Repetitive routine work has to be done. The danger is that one gradually loses touch with the source. The daily routine takes over.

13 / The False Economy Dragon

"When the motive is right, the need is expressed, the money will come—so let's start." John knows someone who can install the central heating and Peter has found some furniture and we can live with the bank loan. One hears the "false economy dragon" laughing. When midwinter comes, the pipes burst, the furniture falls to pieces, and the school has to close for a few weeks.

14 / The Bursar Dragon

"We can only spend when the money is received." "We haven't budgeted for this, so we cannot do it." The danger of this dragon is that every initiative is killed before it is born because there is no money.

These dragons can be placed in pairs and related to the seven aspects described in chapter 1.

1/RECOGNIZING THE MOTIVE

The Disintegration Dragon   ↔   The Sect Dragon

2/ANSWERING THE NEED

The Subsidy Dragon   ↔   The Autonomy Dragon

3/FORMULATING DIRECTION

The Adapting Dragon   ↔   The Model Dragon

4/COMMITMENT OF PEOPLE

The Delegation Dragon   ↔   The Solo Dragon

5/WORKING TOGETHER

The Hurry Dragon   ↔   The Expansion Dragon

6/MANAGING PROCESSES AND TIME

The Dilettante Dragon   ↔   The Routine Dragon

7/FINDING RESOURCES AND FACILITIES

The False Economy Dragon   ↔   The Bursar Dragon

Many of these dragons surround an initiative and they will make use of any weaknesses. At the same time they are the development helpers—just like childhood illnesses—of the initiative.

This picture of the dragons can be used as a diagnostic tool by the coworkers to enable them to become clear about the challenges that face them. It might be helpful to spend an evening together looking at the one-sidedness of one's initiative and discussing how consciousness and balance can be brought into the situation.

5

Ways of Working Together in the Developing Organization

TŸNO VOORS AND

CHRISTOPHER SCHAEFER

The healing social life is only found when in the mirror of the human soul the whole community finds its reflection and when in the community the virtue of each soul is living.

Rudolf Steiner, the motto of the Social Ethic

When an initiative starts, a small carrying group tends to make many decisions quickly and informally. In starting a school, a small parent group will meet periodically over supper and decide issues of hiring, name, and location in a series of quick conversations. A new store in Montreal received its beginning and initial impetus from discussions between a young couple who grabbed whatever time was available to work out the myriad decisions needed for a new enterprise. However, even in this exciting childhood period of initiatives, it is important for initiative-takers to draw distinctions between different types of issues and, whenever possible, to create meetings that primarily address one area of decision-making so that a hodgepodge of issues does not produce excessive tiredness and irritation.

We saw that organizations, like individuals, have an identity that comes to expression in the central goals of the initiative, in its philosophy, name, approach to customers, and in its advertising material. The small store in Montreal became La Futonerie and was dedicated to the manufacture and sale of high quality, custom made, natural fiber futons (bedding). A new school became the Lexington Waldorf School because it was based on the principles of Waldorf education. Initiative-takers need to create special meetings in which questions of identity can be discussed, in which the vision of the initiative and the needs of customers and clients can be explored.

Such meetings in which the mission of the initiative is nurtured can best be organized a few times a year as work days or as *conference meetings* involving everyone connected with the initiative.

A different type of meeting that needs to take place more frequently, once a week or at least twice a month, is the *coworkers' staff meeting*. Here the social dimension of the initiative is discussed. Questions of hiring, work conditions, salary questions, task divisions will be debated and then decided upon by the carrying group.

Meetings devoted to the everyday work of the initiative, or work group or committee meetings again have a different quality. Tasks need to be coordinated on a daily and a weekly basis; the ordering of supplies, the review of accounts, and the checking of orders need to take place. While such meetings will differ in content between a school, a restaurant, and a small manufacturing plant they are highly specific in nature, and involve those who are directly connected to specific tasks.

The first kind of meeting, the *conference*, in essence entails a dialogue with the spirit of the initiative, the second, the *work meeting*, a dialogue among coworkers, and the third a dialogue with the earth—with money, resources, and administrative questions.

Even in the beginning years of the initiative these distinctions are important to begin working on so that there can be an adequate focus and time for each main area of organizational life.

The Conference: Working on Identity Questions

Conference or Work Days have the function of allowing reflection on the essential questions facing initiatives. Such meetings, lasting a number of days, allow review of the past, surfacing of present issues, and rededication to a common future. Whether the initiative is new or already well established, such a review of the past and a discussion of the future is vital to the institution's health. It is like our own need as individuals to occasionally step back from the pressures of everyday life in order to see what is essential in our lives and what new directions are called for.

It is important that such meetings or conferences develop a rhythm, a regularity in the course of the year. Strength is built on repetition. For many of the initiatives we have worked with, an annual or semi-annual conference or retreat was the only opportunity individuals had to explore basic questions and, equally vital, to get to know each other better as people. Such meetings should be open to all who are involved in the initiative. In the case of a school it should involve teachers, board members, administrative staff, and parents who demonstrated an ongoing commitment to the school by serving on committees or carrying out other school responsibilities. Other institutions such as counseling or therapy centers, consultancy organizations, or architects find such work days can involve not only professional staff but also support staff, advisory board members, and occasionally family members and valued clients. The same holds true of smaller service organizations.

In arranging such meetings it is often good to leave the usual workplace and find an inexpensive retreat center, a farm or some other location in which individuals can relax while reviewing the central questions of their work life.

Since, in most cases, such conferences or retreats cover one or more days, a balance of activities should be sought. In our work with clients, we recommend some artistic activity in the morning after breakfast (singing, movement, sculpture, painting), followed either by a common study, or a talk by an outside person knowledgeable about a field that is of interest to the initiative, or a prepared talk by someone in the carrying group. Then there can be time for discussing some of the central questions that the initiative faces; for example:

Why did enrollment decrease in our school last year? How can we improve teacher/parent relationships? Why is our consultancy company only attracting service or cultural institutions as clients? How can we become more visible in our community as a whole-food café? Why is there a lack of commitment in our organization? How can we improve our meetings and improve the mood among staff? Can we develop a renewed image of the future that articulates our values and priorities?

The discussion of such questions is best held in groups of twelve or fewer so that individuals have the opportunity to speak and to be heard. Such a division into groups. however, then requires a common sharing in the whole circle.

Then comes lunch and a digestive walk or some physical work. It is surprising how conducive repair work, raking leaves, or gardening can be to heart-to-heart talks. Further discussion in groups can take place in the afternoon, followed by an enjoyable supper. The evening is best spent in social activity, music, storytelling, or reading. Occasionally an inspirational talk for everyone can also energize reflection and encourage sleep.

The idea behind work days or a conference meeting is less to make practical decisions than to form a picture of present issues and future possibilities and to help enliven a vision of the initiative and its mission in the world. Issues will need further discussion and decision in project groups and committees.

Periodic conference or retreat meetings of this type are vital to the health of all types of institutions, because they contribute to regeneration and development.

LEVELS OF LISTENING

Helps and Hindrances

To be effective listeners, we must learn to listen to the whole person—not just to the words he/she is saying, but also to what lies between or behind the actual words.

We need to listen to thoughts, feelings, and intentions.

"Head listening"
to facts, concepts, arguments, ideas.

"Heart listening"
to emotions, values, mood, experience.

"Listening to the will"
energy, direction, motivation.

THE THINKING LEVEL : Head Listening

The most obvious way to listen—apparently "objective"—but not as effective as we imagine. Can we truly follow with our own thoughts, the thoughts of the speaker? We think much faster than he/she speaks—how do we use this extra mental time—to synthesize and digest what we are hearing, or to think our own separate thoughts?

Hindrances on this level include problems of attention and accuracy, but also arise from the different frames of reference held by speaker and listener. Our knowledge, concepts, vocabulary, and way of thinking derive from the past—our own individual past education and experience. If we do not allow for the fact that the other person has his own, perhaps very different, frame of reference, it is all too easy to get our wires crossed, or to assume a level of understanding that is not real. We continually run the danger of overcomplicating or oversimplifying what we hear.

The listening process is supported on this level by the cultivation of a genuine interest in "where the other person is coming from"—an open-minded approach that does not judge his/her words according to my preconceptions.

THE FEELING LEVEL : Heart Listening

Listening on this level means penetrating a step deeper into the other's experience—apparently rational statements may be covering feelings of distress, anger, or embarrassment. These may be heard more through the tone of voice, facial expressions, or a gesture, than in what is actually said, and can be obscured, especially if we are unaccustomed to, or inhibited about, expressing feelings directly.

Accurate perception of feelings is continually impaired by the effects of our own feelings, the likes and dislikes that arise in us semiconsciously in the face of certain people, situations, or issues. Even the mention of certain "trigger" words or phrases can call up quite strong emotions in us, which obscure our perception of what the other is feeling. Effective listening can be fostered on the feeling level by "quietening" our own reactions to the immediate impressions we receive, and developing the quality of empathy. This means allowing ourselves calmly to "live into" the other person's experience as he/she is speaking. The faculty of social sensibility that can be trained in this way is a key attribute of skilled negotiators.

THE WILL LEVEL : Intentional Listening

To sense the real intentions of another person can be one of the hardest aspects of the art of listening. Often, speakers are themselves only dimly aware of what they actually want in a situation. Skillful listening can help to discover, "behind" the thoughts and "below" the feelings involved, the real sources of potential energy and commitment. This will often involve sensing what is left unsaid. The future lies asleep in people's will-forces.

One impulse of the will that is only too quick to awaken is the urge toward power and conflict, to impose my own will and resist the other person's. Resistance at the level of intention is often rationalized into arguments that can never be resolved, because the basic will to reach agreement is not present. If I allow these adversarial forces to arise in me while listening, I create an immediate barrier to a creative future work-relationship.

If I can hold back "my way" of acting in the situation, and continually look for elements of common direction and mutuality, I may be able to open the way toward future cooperation.

INEFFECTIVE LISTENING

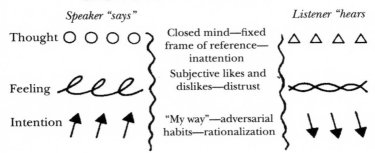

EFFECTIVE LISTENING

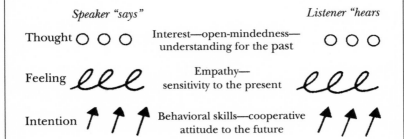

Active effective listening on these three levels will be a substantial, creative contribution in many realms of social and professional life.

EXERCISE

Listening on Three Levels

AIM: To practice skills of listening in the following ways:

1. Accuracy and attention in relation to the information, ideas, and mental pictures actually expressed by the speaker.

2. Sensitivity to the underlying feelings and mood, which may or may not be directly expressed.

3. Recognizing the fundamental direction of the speaker's intentions and energy.

METHOD:

Groups of four. One person relates a recent experience that contains a certain problem or question for him/her, which is still open or unresolved. Each listener takes one level.

After the speaker has finished and a brief pause for reflection, the listeners are asked to share their observations in the following ways respectively:

1. Retell in your own words the main elements of the story you heard. What facts and concepts did the speaker use to make that situation clear?

2. Describe the feelings you imagine were present in the speaker:
   a) in the past situation that was described.
   b) during the telling.

3. What kinds of motivation could you perceive in the speaker? What does/did he/she want to do about the situation described? How much commitment and energy is present, and in what directions?

All observations are then checked with the storyteller. How accurate was the listening? What was missed? Did the feedback make the speaker more aware of certain semiconscious factors? Distinguish between observation and interpretation—how justified was the latter?

Repeat with new tellers—possible also with listeners all taking all levels, building up feedback together on each.

The Carrying Group or Core Group Meeting

The coworkers who are able and willing to carry responsibility for the whole of the initiative should meet regularly. This meeting focuses on the aims of the initiative, on coordination of tasks, and on organizational and policy questions. This group will, for example, have to develop and review the approach to customers, to new products, and to publicity. They will need to discuss personnel questions and policies on salaries for part-time and full-time workers as well as questions of tuition or price. They will also regularly look at central tasks and the division of responsibilities. It is advisable to have these meetings fairly regularly, perhaps once a week. In new initiatives the question of who should be part of these meetings arises. The answer is those who both feel responsible and have demonstrated their commitment to the initiative and its aims. Being there at least a year or more is vital so that one understands the culture, mood, and work life of the institution.

The nature and atmosphere of the carrying group meeting are different from those of the conference. One will always experience the pressure of time in these meetings. The agenda is often long, and a lot of information is exchanged that needs to be weighed and judged. Sometimes quite different points of view have to be brought together and strong differences of opinion will arise. In the carrying group meetings, one exercises the *art of balance*, of give and take, of breathing together. The secret, the heart of the meeting, lies in the fact that everyone can speak, that everyone can experience being heard, and that a sense of mutual equality and dedication arises. This process of working together takes time and is a process of joint learning. A careful preparation of meetings, an agreed-upon process of decision-making, and a review of meetings are essential.

The agenda of the meeting needs to be clear to members of the group beforehand so that an inner preparation is possible. We have all experienced the dilemma of arriving at meetings, breathless from our last task, with not a clue about what is going to be discussed. So everyone needs to have some idea of what is coming toward them, preferably in the form of a brief agenda noting the issues to be discussed and something of their relative priority. New issues can of course be added as the agenda is reviewed at the beginning of the meeting.

For the carrying group, short minutes are also important so that issues discussed, decided upon, and delegated to someone for implementation can be reviewed. Without such minutes, it is easy to forget what was agreed to and even easier to forget what you were supposed to do between one meeting and the next.

Approaches to decision-making and suggestions for the review of meetings will be discussed later in this chapter.

Work or Committee Meetings

The third kind of meeting to be held regularly is the work meeting, such as finance or publicity. The daily work must be done with care. Activities must be coordinated and work processes planned. Supplies, materials, and other resources need to be available at the right moment. The bookkeeping, payment of bills, salaries, and monthly financial reviews must be carried out. In every initiative and organization the need to divide tasks among smaller work teams or individuals is readily apparent. In schools there are questions of admissions, parent interviews, publicity, scheduling, bookkeeping, maintenance, and the ordering of supplies. In smaller production facilities, the needs of marketing, sales, ordering, shipment, production, quality control, and accounting are easily seen and need the attention of one or more individuals.

In dividing work tasks, areas of responsibility need to be clearly defined and reviewed. Short daily meetings are often necessary to inform each other, to coordinate, and to plan and review the work. When the initiative grows, an administrative group will meet regularly and the work meetings will take place within the different sections or work teams.

In work meetings, decisions about work activities need to be made quickly and on the spot. Delegation must be cultivated so that individuals are free to act in their areas of responsibility. It is in the realm of the deed that our work interdependence and co-responsibility become apparent. If the food is not ordered for the café the cook cannot function, and if a teacher is in a bad mood and poorly prepared on a given day the other teachers will experience the consequences in later lessons.

For many of us, being truly responsible is difficult, especially when we are functioning as equals in a new initiative. It is clearer, and, of course, more compelling if we have a boss. Yet the opportunity for exercising free responsibility, recognizing our interdependence and developing mutual trust is one of the challenges of working collegially, a challenge that will stretch us inwardly and help us develop new social faculties.

There will, of course, be other kinds of committees and project groups that initiatives will need, but the conference, the carrying group, and work teams represent the three basic joint activities required of any initiative. Without such a dialogue of the head, the heart, and the hand neither the individual nor the institution can work freely and effectively. While all three types of meetings are important for the different types of initiatives, the work or task group meeting is more central for product organizations, the carrying group or policy and procedure meeting for service institutions, and the conference or identity meeting for cultural initiatives.

TEAM MEETING CHARACTERISTICS

Weekly (or regular) Agenda • Recording decisions • Review the meeting • Planning next meeting

THE TEAM INCLUDES

A leader • A scribe/recorder • A timekeeper • Team members • A facilitator

TEAM LEADER CHARACTERISTICS

Responsibility • Preparation • Punctuality • Ability to maintain order • Eye contact • Good communication • Appropriate gestures • Non-apologetic • Enthusiastic

WHEN DOES A GROUP BECOME A TEAM?

When they can focus on common issues or problems • When leadership arises • When they are motivated to accomplish something • When the participation level increases • When communications deepen, there is active listening • When a "common language" arises • When trust or interdependence grows • When there is consensus decision making • When there is progress toward an agreed upon goal • When a common identity grows

THE TEAM LEADER'S ROLE IN MEETINGS

Know the issues before the beginning • Prepare and circulate an agenda • Announce each topic and time frame • Ask for input, balance participation • Follow agenda and keep discussion on track • Insure participants get to finish • Summarize what has been decided • Ask for decisions and suggests conclusions

THE GROUP MEMBER'S ROLE IN MEETINGS

Have a clear and shared agenda • Have goals or objectives • Listen to one another • Speak clearly and concisely • Allow adequate participation—space • Build on other's contributions • Summarize • Review the meeting briefly for common learning

The Mandate Organization

As an initiative grows in size, the initial carrying group or the coworkers' meeting has increased difficulties in dealing with the many issues requiring decision and action. Delegation and a differentiation of tasks is required to help the initiative continue to prosper.

At this point two obstacles appear. One is a democratic tendency in which it is maintained that we have to decide everything together. The result is endless meetings, long agendas, and much discussion without much action. In some schools in which we have worked the collegium or coworkers meeting regularly had twenty to twenty-five items to discuss in a single meeting, including disciplinary action against an individual child, Christmas fair publicity, class trip questions, financial requests for conference attendance, and how to look for a new French teacher. Many of these issues should be worked on by individuals and small committees, yet everyone wants to feel involved.

The other obstacle is an autocratic or oligarchic tendency in which one or two workhorses do most of the work and wield the power behind the scenes. Neither tendency is healthy for the initiative, because it hides the real need to establish a "republican"[1] mandate structure in which the variety of tasks necessary for the running of the school, the shop, or the therapeutic center is clearly delegated or mandated to individuals or small groups. Such delegation implies that an individual or a committee is given the mandate to make decisions on behalf of the whole organization in clearly defined areas of work.

The creation of a mandate system in an organization, above all, requires clarity and trust. Clarity through having a shared vision of the aims and purposes of the organization, and also clarity about its policies and decision-making procedures. The

---

1. Ernst Lehrs, *Republican, Not Democratic* (Fair Oaks, CA: AWSNA).

conference or work days are vital as an ongoing part of the initiative's life in order to achieve such clarity and renew the shared vision. Developing a mandate system suggests a transformation of the coworkers' meeting from the space in which all important decisions are decided to the space in which mainly policies are made and mandates allocated. Policies are guiding principles—such as what kind of coworkers are we looking for, what is our salary system or policy, what guidelines do we have on scholarships, and what image and qualities do we wish to project in our fairs and publicity material. If there are clear policies in the areas of pricing, personnel, research, publicity, and the like, then an individual or a committee is capable of making decisions for the whole.

In establishing a mandate system the initiative and the mandate holders need to be aware of the following principles:

- The area of responsibility must be clearly defined by the carrying group meeting and regularly reviewed.
- The mandate holder (or committee) is autonomous in making decisions within their designated mandate area.
- The mandates are held for a limited period of time, usually for 1 or 2 years, or a maximum of 3 years.
- Mandate holders may take a specific decision to the carrying group meeting in case of uncertainty or gravity of consequence. Such a step does not mean that they are giving up their mandate but only seeking guidance.
- Carrying group meetings need to take place regularly to enable mandate holders to listen carefully to the information, ideas, opinions, and feelings that are expressed and to clarify policy questions.

WAINWRIGHT RECEPTIVE LISTENING

Guidelines for Effective Group Participation

1. Listen with Trust

I will have faith in the process of growth and I will keep in mind that each of us has the answers within.

I will not take responsibility for another person's comfort or growth by giving advice, minimizing, preaching, probing or analyzing.

2. Listen with empathy and love

I will listen from within the speaker's experience to what he or she is saying and feeling, and I will acknowledge, with or without words, that he or she is being heard.

I will not argue or question each person's right to express opinions contrary to mine.

3. Listen with patience

I will allow a suitable interval of silence between speakers, taking in what was said, and listening to the wisdom within.

I will not interrupt, nor share my own experience until I have fully heard the other person's experience, if then.

4. Speak from "I"

I will respond from my own experience, feelings and opinions rather than use my intellect to debate the content of a person's sharing.

I will not disown my experience by quoting authorities or by generalizing with "we," "you," or "never."

5. Share the floor

I will accept personal responsibility for fostering participation of every other group member by limiting my speaking time to a proportionate share of the total time.

6. Maintain confidentiality

I will respect what has been shared with the group as confidential.

I will not bring up another's sharing outside the session—to the speaker or to others.

Used by the Board of Wainwright House in Rye, N.Y.

An understanding and mutual listening between the mandate group members and the carrying group meeting is a precondition for the maintenance of trust in the organization. The mandate holders make decisions that often influence the work situations of their colleagues. The basis for a willingness to accept and execute decisions of a committee or a mandate holder lies in the mutual acceptance of the mandate principles, and the daily experience that the trust given to the mandate holder is used in a healthy way. The readiness with which co-workers accept decisions—even when one has a differing opinion about the specific situation—is an essential aspect of a collegial way of working. In this sense mandating means learning to accept the others' specific talents, their one-sidedness, and their judgements. Through a mandate structure one practices mutual acceptance and collegiality as well as creating a more efficient work organization.

One of the most delicate aspects of creating a delegation system based on clear mandates is the question of the selection and appointment of mandate holders. One way of approaching this issue is through the principle of co-option. The committee or the individual mandate holder thereby accepts the task of finding a successor or successors. If this way is chosen by the initiative then the following procedures are helpful:

- The mandate holders decide to transfer or pass on their specific mandate to a new group.
- The functioning of the mandate or of the committee is reviewed by the coworkers, collegium, or policy-making body and the mandates are again discussed.
- The mandate holders look for successors who they feel possess the capability of carrying out the designated tasks efficiently and well.
- The suggested names are mentioned in the carrying group meeting and an open conversation takes place with the suggested members of the new committee as

well as of the old. Out of this conversation it can be
seen whether the new group has the confidence of the
coworkers or whether a different individual or individuals are required.
- The new mandate holders are then appointed by the
old. In this way a new publicity committee, a financial
planning group, or a parent contact person can be
selected for a school.

A modification of the co-option principle is for the carrying
group meeting to select new mandate holders on the basis of
the recommendation of the previous group. However, what is
important is not to fall into the trap of volunteerism. Some
schools and educational institutions delegate tasks mainly on
the basis of who is willing to do the job. This can result in the
least capable people doing a task. It is, after all, very difficult to
say "no" to someone in a volunteer system. For work to be done
well competence is required. Unfortunately we are not very
able to judge our own levels of skill and competence and need
the help of colleagues in seeing our strengths and weaknesses.

In any mandate structure it is important to set clear time lim-
its for a certain group carrying out the mandate and equally to
let them carry it out without interference. Except in cases of
gross negligence, the mandate should not be recalled or termi-
nated except at the request of the mandate holders.

As an initiative develops and begins to delegate or mandate
tasks, the question of who should be on the policy-making body
or the carrying-group meeting arises. Initially, everyone, part-
or full-time people, may have been part of the initiative group.
But now the need for continuity and commitment becomes
important, for the carrying-group is the heart and the guiding
organ of the initiative. It is this group, often referred to as a
College of Teachers in Waldorf schools, which needs the
insight and strength to understand the totality of the initiative,
to nurture it and to guide it into the future.

We have looked at three basic meetings in an initiative: the conference connected to goals and to the mission of the organization; the carrying-group meeting for developing the guiding principles and policies; and the work or committee meetings for carrying out specific tasks. This division gives one an insight into criteria for membership in the coworkers group, collegium, or policy-making body. In our experience, three types of questions are important to discuss with potential new members of the carrying group:

1. Do they inwardly share the goals and philosophy of the organization? In other words, do they feel connected to the mission of the organization? (Spiritual Community)
2. Do they feel humanly connected to their colleagues? Are they perceived as fitting into the "social community" of the initiative? (Social Community)
3. Do they manifest sufficient professional competence to be part of the permanent work community? (Work Community)[2]

It is usually best to make such criteria visible to potential members of the coworkers group or collegium and to allow individuals to request membership after one or more years in the organization. Once they have requested to join they can address these questions in the full circle of colleagues and be asked questions by the others. After such a discussion, the existing coworker's group can then decide whether membership is appropriate for the person or persons in question.

It is best not to keep criteria for membership hidden and to select some people and not others on the basis of a process that is invisible to the faculty as a whole. In some Waldorf schools membership in the collegium is experienced as a

---

2. See chapter 3.

highly political and hidden process in which favoritism abounds. Clarity of procedure and criteria of membership avoid unnecessary speculation and ill will.

In developing a mandate organization it becomes important to have a *coordinating group* that plans the coworkers meeting and coordinates activities within the initiative. This group needs to be well informed about the different mandate areas. Its coordination function is of central importance for the nurturing of good communication, and must be seen as a separate mandate. The coordination group is not the executive of the initiative but rather a facilitating, communication, and planning organ.

A further condition for a proper functioning of the mandate structure is a salary arrangement that is in agreement with the collegial model described. No financial consequences are attached to the execution of mandate functions. The mandate structure should be seen as a situational, ever-moving form of working together. In other words, a leadership that can change according to the situation.

A good example of a mandate organization is ARTA in Holland. ARTA is a therapeutic center where people suffering from drug addiction can be helped. In 1980, this initiative with 15 coworkers chose to change its hierarchical structures to a new republican structure, in which decision-making was mandated to one or more coworkers. They formed a carrying group of coworkers and created the following mandate areas:

- *Admission mandate.* This mandate group was responsible for developing the admission policy of future residents and became responsible for its implementation.
- *Personnel mandate.* This mandate group, generally responsible for selection, acceptance, and dismissal of coworkers, was responsible for the description of the different work functions of the coworkers and the individual development questions of the coworkers.

- *Financial mandate.* This mandate group was responsible for developing a more conscious relation to money among the coworkers.
- *Therapy mandate.* This mandate group was responsible for all therapeutic aspects of the ARTA program.

ARTA also has mandates for maintenance, timetabling, external relations, after care, and the very important mandate responsibility of guiding and coordinating development of this new structure of decision-making.

In addition to the mandates for aspects of the organization that embrace more than one function, everyone in ARTA has responsibility for his or her own function. In ARTA there are craftsmen or specialists responsible for the professional running of the work areas, finance, administration, garden, kitchen, wood workshop, weavery, and so on. There are also team members and personal counselors. A doctor, a psychiatrist, and many different art therapists have a part-time relation to ARTA, but have no specific responsibility in the organization.

Many Waldorf schools and other educational and volunteer organizations have a well-developed committee structure that can be transformed into a mandate system by a more conscious articulation of mandates. This process of articulation involves achieving greater clarity about policies and procedures by the coworkers meeting followed by a common definition of mandate tasks. Such a step is advisable for many of the organizations we work with so that a coordination of tasks takes place and so that the many issues of trust among colleagues can be ameliorated through a conscious set of organizational principles and procedures.

In this chapter we have not discussed the question of boards of directors or other legal questions largely because of the differences in legal codes between different English-speaking countries. In both U.S. and Canadian schools, some mandates or committees will be connected to the board, such as finance, development, building and grounds, and perhaps publicity. The mandating principles are important, whether the mandating group is the college of teachers, the coworkers meeting, or a board of directors.

Working Together in Groups

Working together in groups has the same intimate relation to the image of the human being as organizational forms. One can, for example, distinguish between three fundamental types of groups. There are *study groups* whose aim is to help the individual members arrive at a more complete understanding of a text or subject; *social groups* whose aim is to work on human relationships; and *work groups,* which are task directed.[3] The first primarily focuses on our thought capacities, the second on our feeling life, while the third calls upon our will.

While this section will deal primarily with work groups, it is important to recognize that the dynamics of all groups are characterized by elements connected to the three souls capacities of the human being. We exchange ideas, concepts, and information through words. This content level of group life is strongly connected to our thought life. In addition there is the quality of relationships, the weaving of sympathies and antipathies between group members. This level of feelings is often less visible than the content level but is no less important. I may not agree with another person's idea simply because he or she cut me off less than five minutes ago. Thirdly, there is the will life of the group, the common aims and procedures that we follow or don't follow during our discussions.[4]

---

3. See Bernard Lievegoed, *Towards the 21st Century, Doing the Good* (Toronto: Steiner Book Centre, 1972), 56–75. For a more complete description of different types of groups. See also Martin Large, *Social Ecology*, 42–58.
4. See Large, *Social Ecology*, 42–58.

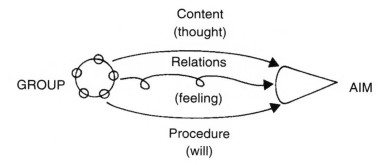

Content
(thought)

GROUP

Relations
(feeling)

AIM

Procedure
(will)

Most working groups are relatively conscious of content, less conscious of relationships, and least conscious of procedure. Yet this last area is one of the most essential for initiatives if they are to make effective use of their time and to arrive at collegial decisions. All too often the procedural aspect of group life is neglected with the result that there is limited clarity about the group's aims, its agenda, and its process of decision-making.

In focusing on procedure, the first essential ingredient for a fruitful meeting is planning. Has the agenda been prepared and sent out to members? Are the aims of the discussion clear? Which issues need decisions, which analysis? What information is required? How much time should be allocated to each topic?

These questions can be briefly reviewed and discussed at the start of the meeting and new items added to the agenda if necessary. An important distinction to be aware of in the planning phase of the discussion is the difference between problem-solving and decision-making. For example, the question of how the grading policy in the high school is working is a problem-solving question. It is past directed and involves investigation and analysis. The question of what kind of new grading policy should be adopted is a decision-making question directed toward the future and involves the exploration of alternative options.

Typically the planning phase of a meeting is followed by some information sharing, by judging and weighing, and then arriving at a conclusion or a decision.

Planning

What agenda items? How much time? Aims of the discussion?
(decisions, conclusions, sharing). Sequence of items and discussion?

| *Problem Solving* | *Decision Making* |
| (Past Directed) | (Future Directed) |

Information Sharing

What is our grading policy?
What are our profit margins
or losses?
When did the child leave
the school and why?

Information Sharing

What alternative grading
policies or pricing structures are
possible?
What are the ways in which
we can avoid losing children from
the school unnecessarily?

(Light of thinking—information)

Judging—Weighing

What are the most relevant
facts in this situation?
Why is the grading policy
inadequate?
According to what values
and criteria are we judging?

Judging—Weighing

What are the consequences of the
different alternatives?
What principles make one more
preferable than the other?

(Feelings—Values)

Conclusion

Our present grading policy
is inadequate.
Our profit margins are
too low.
The child was not
handled properly (or she
was handled adequately
by teacher).

Decision

We will only begin giving letter
grades in tenth grade.
All cosmetic products need a
profit margin of 90% before being
sold to distributors.
All grave disciplinary cases will be
reviewed by a committee before a
child is dismissed.

(Will—Conclusions—Decisions)

If a group, over time, learns to work creatively with a common procedure such as the one described, then collegial decisions will be much easier. However, too much emphasis on procedure kills the life of the meeting, so a sense of balance between procedural consciousness and lively engagement needs cultivation. Generally speaking, the larger the group the more form and consciousness is required to produce a fruitful outcome.

The chairperson carries a primary responsibility for seeing that a reasonable procedure is adhered to in a meeting. He or she will also need to guide the interaction—the rhythm of speaking and listening—so that confusion, sub-conversations or repeated interruptions can be avoided.

The more mature and developed a group is the less leadership will be required by a chairperson. However, such development only occurs if a periodic review of the meeting takes place so that a collective awareness of both procedural and interaction patterns can be born. Adults learn most effectively through reflecting on experience. A review or evaluation of group process is an essential tool in bringing about a heightened awareness of what goes on in groups and how the process of working together can be improved. Short evaluations can be held after each coworkers' meeting or for a longer time on a periodic basis, for example, every third or fourth meeting. Types of questions to be explored include:

CONTENT Were our contributions to the point? How was the balance between information and ideas or concepts? Did we discuss the subject(s) adequately?

INTERACTION How was the balance between speaking and listening? Did contributions build on each other? Did individuals feel cut off by others? How was the mood of the discussion? How can we improve our listening? How did the chairperson function?

PROCEDURE   Was our agenda clear? Did we achieve our aims? How was our time awareness? Was the judgement process dealt with satisfactorily? How was the sequence of problem-solving and decision-making? Have past decisions been carried out?

Questions such as these stimulate reflection and awareness. A group may appoint an observer to help guide the review process, but it is important that the group itself reviews rather than that the observer pronounces judgements. It is also important to keep in mind that as much can be learned from what went well as from what didn't.

An additional benefit of evaluation is that it can help the group to build loyalty. After any meeting a review takes place but in the corridors or on the way home. Sitting with friends we tend to give vent to our feelings. An opportunity to do this responsibly in the full circle will over time give a new substance to the meetings as well as decrease the tendency toward irresponsible gossip.

Conclusion

In this chapter we have indicated some principles for working together in initiatives and given suggestions for creating collegial forms. Central to our perspective is the idea that initiatives are human creations based on an image of the human being. By making such an image explicit we have tried to show how a threefold picture of the human being can both illuminate and give form to ways of working together collegially. All initiatives are involved in a dialogue with the spirit (aims, values, vision) with the human soul world (customers, clients, coworkers) and with the earth (buildings, machines, resources). Developing and maintaining these dialogues is one precondition of organizational health. The other is finding those forms capable of enhancing the creativity, dedication, enthusiasm, and social responsibility of ourselves as coworkers and colleagues.

6

Funding Initiatives

STEPHEN BRIAULT AND

WARREN ASHE

Money will come to you when you are doing the right thing.
Michael Phillips

1. Money as Problem and Challenge

Every new project wishing to find its place in social life will meet the necessity of obtaining and effectively handling finance. In some cases this challenge will be met from the outset; in other projects, especially where the aims are primarily social and cultural rather than economic, there may be a certain reluctance to enter consciously into this realm. Quite often financial responsibility devolves onto one or two individuals in the initiative. This isolation can become a considerable burden for such people; it can also become an apparent or real source of power within the project. Many institutions striving to bring something new and worthwhile in social life show a constant struggle and insecurity in the financial realm, and this can undermine great human efforts and sacrifices.

To overcome these dangers, ways of understanding and handling money will need to be developed, which can be accessible to all those involved, so as to free the carriers of the initiative from the paralysis and feelings of helplessness that often surround this field. Working with finances must be seen as an integral part of the initiative process; through money a project finds and sustains its earthly "body" in social life. The financial profile of an organization expresses in abstract form how far and in what way the initiative has been able to "find its feet."

This chapter will offer some perspectives on the way in which money moves and acts in social life and in organizations, and derive from these perspectives a number of principles for the management of the capital and the revenue aspects of financing initiatives. It will also describe a range of experiences gained through trying to work in new ways with money, and introduce the aims and methods of Mercury Provident Society, itself a significant new initiative in the field of banking.

2. The Threefold Nature of Social Life and of Finance

The initiators of any enterprise need to use wealth to bring it to life. This requirement applies to a garden plot or a research project, a church or a motor manufacturer. If the initiators do not have enough wealth of their own, they will need access to others' wealth. The *social* character of the undertaking will be in part determined by the immediate source and the form of that wealth. However, it is the essential *functional* character of the enterprise that will determine the nature of the wealth needed to launch it.

There are three primary functions or purposes that may be discerned in human enterprises. The first we may term economic. Any undertaking supplying saleable material, goods, or services to meet consumer demand is primarily economic. A retail shop, an airline, a structural engineering firm, and a pig farm are all examples of this kind of activity; they are commercial and industrial because their purpose is to serve bodily needs: to make goods accessible, to transport people and goods, to guide and improve the construction of buildings, and to produce food, respectively. Their funding ultimately is to be met from the proceeds of their goods or the charges made for their services. If they are consistently unprofitable, there may be good reason to dismantle them. (The practice of subsidizing an economic activity is simply using the profits of other units in the economy to enable unprofitable units to continue, rightly or wrongly.) If they are profitable, they may grow or they may benefit financially those who own them or have capitalized them. But in the end their continued existence depends on the *profitable* provision of goods and services to consumers. The exchange taking place in their transactions provides the wealth they depend on.

A second category of human social activities we may call political. By "political" is meant those areas of action that directly deal with civic equality and rights, that is, the processes of lawmaking, of law enforcement and execution, and of jurisprudence. The boundaries of legitimate governmental action are, of course, a matter of intense debate, and need not concern us here. The point is that they apply to every citizen equally, and thus are funded by all equally, in the form of taxes. This is not to say that each citizen pays an equal amount, but that the same criteria of levy apply; no individual may evade payment as a citizen in the way he may refrain from expenditure as a consumer of products in commercial-industrial life. In return, the state is uniformly zealous in guarding the rights of each citizen, rich or poor. There is an implied political contract between the state and the individual, just as there was a social contract amongst peasants, priests, and nobility in feudal Europe. (The fact that this contract is so often broken or distorted by both parties does not detract from its validity or from the fact that it is recognized as true by most minds in the world, even though the notion of what constitutes rights is a matter of fundamental disagreement.) The wealth in the form of taxes that changes hands under the political contract does not generate profit.

The third type of intention that may inform human activity is cultural-spiritual. The doctor, the teacher, the pure research scientist, the artist, and the priest are good examples of bearers of the spiritual life. Their work does not concern itself directly with meeting the material needs of people, nor with establishing the laws that guarantee their rights. They occupy themselves with providing spiritual nourishment, with enlightenment, with the exploration of ideas and feelings in their own right. It will be clear that teachers (except for those in vocational training) and the therapeutic occupations, insofar as they concern themselves with the total human well-being for its own sake, fit this category. This category of activity does not make any direct economic contribution to society, but must be supported by the economy in the form of gifts. (The fact that in much of the world the state now supports or administers education, medicine, much scientific research, and some of the arts, funding them by taxation, does not alter their dependence on the economy; few people would dispute the fact that they are not saleable, if only because they should be freely available.) Cultural-spiritual activity gives to the economic life enhanced human capacities and new insights, but its economic effects are only indirect: if a doctor by his skill enables a worker to be more productive, this does not mean that the doctor is a production worker.[1]

These brief and necessarily incomplete sketches of the three spheres of society—or the three primary colors of human activity—are a necessary framework for thinking about the funding of new enterprises, for the three spheres have their counterparts within each enterprise, and each enterprise functions in all three spheres. The whole reflects the contribution of each part, and each part is a microcosm of the whole. But any enterprise has an *essentially* economic, political, or cultural-spiritual character that derives from the purpose for which it is established and run. Thus, a new school exists to

---

1. Rudolf Mees, *Money for a Better World* (Stroud, U.K.:Hawthorn Press, 1991). Also Michael Phillips, *The Seven Laws of Money* (NY: Random House, 1974).

develop the minds and values of children, a publishing firm to produce and provide books for sale, the government of a nation to codify and enforce the norms of its culture in legislation. This predominate focus in one area is true even though the school is a consumer of economic goods, the publisher must concern himself with employees' rights (their political status within the company), and the government concerns itself with spiritual-cultural ideas in forming policy.

When the essential functional character of a new enterprise is grasped, the strategies of financing can be developed. For initiators of enterprises to approach this problem more effectively, it is necessary to look at the character of money itself, for the character of the funding should match the character of the enterprise.

Our primary experience of money is as "cash in hand" or money in one's pocket, and it is usually connected with a transaction, say, the buying of goods. This kind of transaction takes place to the mutual advantage—providing the price is just—of both vendor and purchaser; the vendor needs the money more than he needs the goods, and the purchaser needs the goods more than he needs the money. Mutuality, whether or not the participants are aware of it, underlies every deal, and the fluctuation in prices and market conditions can be seen as adjustments in the buyer and seller relationships. The money concerned—the purchasing medium—circulates at the same rate at which the production-distribution-consumption cycle moves. We may call money in this aspect *purchase money*.[2] This surplus purchase money is available for other functions. It can become either *loan money* or *gift money*.

Loan money is a temporary surplus over needs; it is placed on loan because its owner sees that it may be required at some

2. "Savings" is a serious misnomer; by this term we usually in fact mean investment capital, since people "save" by putting money with investment institutions such as banks or brokers.

future time but can postpone the spending of it. In the case of company profits,[3] loan money is usually made available until capital expenditure may be necessary. The lender and borrower have a common aim—or at least they bear common responsibility for the consequences of their transaction; if the borrower uses the loan to produce poison gas, the lender is co-responsible for the product, for his help has been indispensable in getting it onto the market.

Gift money has a special character. Unlike purchase money, which is the medium of people seeking mutual advantage, or loan money, which serves to join people in common responsibility, gift money has the effect, if properly handled, of liberating people. Thus, a free donation to a church does not oblige the clergy to please the donor in services or sermons; a free donation to a school does not mean that teachers must follow the educational philosophy favored by the donor. It is frequently the reverse, and rightly so; the donor has confidence in the church or school and follows its lead in matters religious and educational, leaving it free to develop according to its own lights. (This is just the opposite of the producer-consumer relationship where consumer demand determines what is produced.) But it is easier said than done to make a *free* donation, with no strings—not even unexpressed expectations—attached. Free gifts happen most frequently in the case of legacies, but even there the legatee may feel constrained to follow the wishes of a benefactor. To give and receive freely are not easily acquired attributes.[4]

---

3. This is not to say that all profits are of one kind; some may result from the production-consumption cycle, others from speculation or even dishonesty. Nevertheless, insofar as they are surplus to current needs, these monies are available.

4. Rudolf Steiner, *World Economy* (London: Rudolf Steiner Press, 1972), chapter 6, pp. 72–83.

3. Money for Initiatives—Capital Financing and New Directions in Banking

The brief review of the three types of money—purchase, loan, gift—is worth thinking about for anyone undertaking a new initiative because it really describes three different *relationships*. If an enterprise is financed with one type of money, the relationship between it and its supporters will be quite different from the relationship that would arise if another kind of money were used. This relationship will be an objective economic fact and may have nothing to do with the personal relationships among the individuals concerned. Let it be said, however, that there are but few undertakings that are born out of and successfully exist upon the freedom implicit in true gift money. Purchase and loan money reflect mutual advantage and common aims respectively, and each involves contractual obligations. Freedom, of course, is just the opposite of obligation. The apparently unsecured future and the necessity for constant renewal of the relationship between donor and recipient involve hard work and a sense of inspiration that go beyond confidence. Do not build on gifts unless you can muster enduring strength.

Let us now look more closely at the statement that *"the character of the funding should match the essential functional character of the enterprise."*

An economic initiative concerns itself primarily with the buying and selling of goods or services; when it is first established, it needs capital, and the provider of capital—a bank or an investor—will seek to determine whether the buying and selling will be sufficiently profitable to give a return on the capital (in the form of interest or dividends) and to repay it within the specified term. It is a risk, a venture undertaken jointly by capitalizer and entrepreneur; similarly, profits are shared. It is the customers' purchase money that makes a production or trading enterprise profitable, and financial skill resides in the ability to balance costs, prices, capital requirements, and efficient working methods to produce profit without offending human values. No matter how it is achieved, however, the loan is being repaid by the use of purchase money.

A loan to a spiritual-cultural enterprise, on the other hand, cannot rely on profitable handling of purchase money for repayment. It will, if the enterprise wishes to function as a *free* entity, have to receive free gifts to repay its original funding. If the surrounding community can give a free undertaking to donate sufficient funds to repay a loan, the same security can be achieved as when managerial expertise and customer satisfaction combine to make a commercial enterprise profitable. Willingness to donate is, however, quite a different thing from the wish to buy, sell, and trade, and the ability to inspire and attract gifts is a valuable trait in a spiritual-cultural enterprise. It is not, however, the same as salesmanship. The potential donor can only give *freely* if he recognizes in the enterprise and in himself the same spiritual intentions. There must be clarity of awareness as well as warmth of feeling if the giving of funds is to be healthy and reliable. It is all-important, therefore, that those responsible for initiating a school, a church, a youth club, or a hospital should be able to express their aims clearly, and that when it begins to function, the initiative is itself an expression of the same impulse.

Whether an enterprise needs gifts, contractual agreements, or purchase money to sustain its activity, initially it is likely to ask for loan money, and thus it may approach a bank or an organization like the Mercury Provident PLC.[5] Mercury was established in order to find a way of handling loan money that would enhance awareness of the nature of such money and the relationships it creates and manifests. As a licensed deposit-taking institution, Mercury tries to act as a lens between depositor

---

5. Mercury Provident PLC, Orlingbury House, Lewes Rd., Forest Row, Sussex, is active in the United Kingdom. The Rudolf Steiner Foundation, RD 1, Box 147A, Chatham, NY 12037, plays a similar role in the United States.

(lender) and borrower. Depositors are asked to specify to whom they wish to lend their money; a list of borrowers is published, and the skill of the banker consists in helping to make the right match. An important step in this process, however, is the examination of projects seeking loans. For some, loan money is inappropriate; for others, a loan may create more problems than it solves. In any case, Mercury must look at the project with a view to testing its viability, its social health, and its essential character.

The banker must always observe confidentiality, so it is not possible to include here an actual case history, but there are set out below two imaginary case histories amalgamating features of several projects that have come Mercury's way. The details are less important than the central thrust of the investigations, which focus on three areas:

1. The purpose or motive for the existence of the enterprise and the needs that it will serve.
2. The social structure of the undertaking: its legal form and ownership, decision-making processes, and relationship to outside supporters.
3. The financial support—capital, guarantees, gifts, or customers—that it is able to attract.

· · · · · · ·

CASE HISTORY ONE: Henry Smith

The Idea and the People:
Henry Smith came to us with the wish to produce handmade wooden and natural-fiber toys, to be marketed through schools. He was a craftsman in wood himself, aged about 55. He was employed in South London as a skilled cabinetmaker and for the last twenty years or more he had made, purely as a hobby, exquisite and universally admired toys sold at school Christmas

fairs. His wife was equally skilled in sewing and doll-making; it was planned that their new enterprise should be a husband-wife partnership.

The Financial Requirement:
Henry Smith asked for a loan of £8,000 in order to buy a small property and convert it into a workshop with an apartment above. He had some £4,000 of his own and hoped to raise elsewhere a ten-year mortgage of £12,000; the property would cost £21,000 with about £3,000 conversion, much of the converting to be done by Smith himself. Toy manufacture and sales should begin, he thought, within six months of purchase, but the deal had to be closed *immediately* or the opportunity to buy the property would be lost.

Mercury's Response:
We told Smith in the first place that there is no such thing as an immediate loan. Every transaction requires investigation and decisions—by lenders and by himself, the borrower. We began to formulate some questions in order to ascertain motivation, financial support and soundness, and social structure.

The intention was to provide children with imaginatively designed toys. The things he had made were esteemed by Waldorf teachers and would surely find a market—or rather take over a part of the existing market, which was already served by two makers of similarly styled toys.[6] Smith's good intentions might only be achieved at a cost to others. Was the financial package sound at all points? Mercury's investigations with orthodox mortgages revealed that Smith would have trouble getting a 50% mortgage over 10 years, largely because of his age and because of the mixed residential and commercial use

---

6. Waldorf teachers, that is, teachers working in Rudolf Steiner schools, sometimes called Waldorf schools, after the first Waldorf School founded by Steiner in Stuttgart.

of the building. He probably needed more like £20,000 from Mercury; but he had made no provision for his own and his wife's support during the (nonproductive) conversion period of six months. Just to repay £20,000 at 10% per annum interest, with capital repayments spread evenly over the 10 years would require £4,000 in the first year, reducing to £2,200 in the final year. To maintain this loan and to meet overheads and salary requirements would require an immediate turnover of £15,000 to £18,000 per annum. Such a volume of business would mean a six-day working week for the Smiths, with no holiday for the first five years, and would demand a very fast rate of work for a skilled craftsman accustomed to putting time into quality at the expense of quantity. In human terms, a high price to pay. To stretch the loan beyond 10 years—already very long—would take it beyond Smith's sixty-fifth year, which we were not prepared to do in any circumstances.

The character and talents of the people were all-important in coming to a decision. Both Smiths were steady, utterly reliable individuals whose honesty was vouched for from several quarters. But neither had any experience of managing a business: they could not read nor maintain accounts, had given no thought to the legal form of the enterprise, had consulted no lawyer about the transfer of the property, and followed with some difficulty the financial reasoning of the Mercury agents who discussed the matter with them. They just had not considered what was really involved in borrowing and repaying. Their overriding desire was to make a positive and healing contribution to life; alongside their courage in undertaking this was a strong sense of independence. (They had never owned their own property before, a fact of which they were almost ashamed.) Henry Smith's gifts did not include salesmanship, and he knew this; hence he insisted that his sales outlets would have to be Waldorf schools and curative homes with, he believed, a built-in market. He did not see any need for active salesmanship among parents and felt that providing an outlet in a school would not create any significant additional work for anyone. He did not wish to use other outlets and had given no thought to the day when trade might grow to the point where he would need employees or partners.

He had not concerned himself with things like the legal structure of his enterprise, and he conceived of the money as being "in the bank" or "the bank's to lend"; fair enough, in view of the prevailing image of financial institutions, but the Smiths found it hard to think of the legal or financial arrangements as being "socially renewing" or otherwise; to them the only really renewing part of the enterprise was the *design of the toys*. In fact, legal and financial questions rather repelled both the Smiths; they simply wanted to make things with their hands.

The Decision:
Mercury turned down the Smith's request on several grounds:

> a) economic conditions had thinned the market down so much that it was doubtful whether they could get enough income;
> b) their lack of business know-how meant they would need a good deal of costly paid advice, or would need to take some costly crew on board—but clearly the economics of the business would not allow either course.
> c) servicing and repaying the loan, while not crippling, would impose too great a strain;
> d) most important, the entrepreneurs' vision of their task was too narrow to inspire others, too craft-centered and socially unaware to enable them to approach people and ask them to make deposits or supply guarantees as security: they simply saw no real human connection between themselves and the rest of the economy, and nothing the Mercury agents said could make any difference in this respect.

Further Consequences:

The two Mercury agents dealing with this case ventured the view that Henry Smith's (and also, to a lesser degree, Mrs. Smith's) real need was for a change in working environment and for a closer connection between his inner commitments and his work. The problem could only be solved by finding him a new job, preferably with like-minded people. If they had borrowed the money and begun the new enterprise, the Smiths would probably have faced problems that would have made them regret their original impulse. The Mercury agents made some suggestions about alternative employment, and, despite some initial ill feeling, the Smiths followed up the leads; a year or so later Henry seemed happily engaged in new work for an established toymaker, and his wife was undertaking training as a needlework teacher; her training partly funded by gift money from a wealthy individual whom one of the Mercury agents had contacted—on his own initiative—after the refusal of the loan.

· · · · · · ·

CASE HISTORY TWO: The Cathedral Waldorf School

The Idea and the People:

In a medium-sized city in central England, a group of four families, all with children of preschool age, wanted Waldorf education for their children. One of the mothers, Ellen Peters, had been trained as a Waldorf teacher and had a little experience in kindergarten and primary school teaching. The others had heard of Waldorf education from lectures, reading, or personal conversation but had no direct experience of it. They were supported by an older woman who had sent her own child and grandchildren to a Waldorf school, and they established a weekly group meeting to study Waldorf education. It grew to a membership of sixteen and gradually became an initiative group and scraped together enough money to send a young local woman on a one-year training program in Waldorf nursery class education. A modest program of public lectures—about one a month—attracted as many as eighty people in one evening. They got a two-page spread in the local paper and set about raising funds by jumble sales, bring-and-buys, and sponsored runs, but they barely paid for their own activities and the training of their nursery class teacher. They were going to need thousands to buy or build a school, and it was at this point that they approached Mercury. Could they borrow if the need arose? Naturally, a hypothetical question can receive only a hypothetical answer. Basically, it would be depend on the strength of their support, said Mercury.

The Financial Requirements:

A disused school building came on the market for £80,000 about a year after the initiative group had first contacted Mercury. The agents went to see it and discussed its suitability. There were pros and contras, of course, but the main concern from Mercury was security. If the building itself were taken as collateral, Mercury would be in the position of foreclosing should the repayments not be made. This was tantamount to holding the school ransom, for the repayments depended on growth, and if growth were faltering or slow, a crisis could arise. The idea of a Borrowing Community (sometimes called a Loan Alliance) was discussed: if a group of, say, 40 families or individuals could be mustered, each prepared to donate £2,000 plus interest over a period of 5 years (under £10 per week) and to cross-guarantee one another, the loan could be made to the group. The point was made that it would have to be done swiftly, for the building would not stay on the market for long.

Mercury's Investigations:

Our two representatives arranged to meet the *whole* group of parents, and questions revealed the following picture. There were about 25 families in the school, with about 30 children, all aged 4 to 6, in the kindergarten. They had developed a notice-able devotion to the school, and in the course of the evening, whenever the children were mentioned, there was a tone and look of mutuality, of common ground, a sense of reassurance that really they were all one family as far as the good of the children was concerned. When it came to money, however, their separation became evident; it could be seen that people hung back from making a commitment, and later it emerged that there was a significant number of families whose incomes would be severely stretched by school costs and a smaller number who sensed that they might be asked to give more than their fair share. The group heard about the Borrowing Community and, as frequently happens, were not sure they had grasped the notion. The agents repeated it step by step:

1. Each family borrows from Mercury a given sum (say £2,000).
2. This borrowed sum is donated to the school (under Deed of Covenant, using legitimate tax advantages).
3. Each family debt is repaid with interest to Mercury over five years.
4. Mercury's security is a set of cross-guarantees; that is, if there are forty members of the Borrowing Community, each borrowing £2,000, each borrower guarantees to provide 1/40 of every other borrower's debt in the event of default. This means that each borrower *guarantees* £2,000 in addition to *borrowing* £2,000, while his loan is guaranteed by all his fellow borrowers.
5. The whole is handled as one account and one transaction by Mercury, who deals with an individual or small group (as Treasurer) of the Borrowing Community. The Treasurer is responsible for seeing that repayments are made regularly and that communication is alive and well throughout.

There was considerable admiration expressed for the dexterity of this technique, but it was clear that few if any parents were prepared to commit themselves to the Community. The £80,000 building would not be achievable, and the initiative group reconsidered the position. They would not be able to establish any class beyond kindergarten, and there was no way of knowing when such an opportunity would arise again. The initiative group seemed dispirited by the lack of response, but the Mercury agents told them that this was not unusual; in fact, the parents were held together only by their children, not by a common ideal of education or common sense of values. The initiative group would have to see if that much stronger bond was there.

For the next year the search for new premises was therefore not pursued. The emphasis was on the search for common ground among parents; there were more talks and discussion groups, but this time it was the members of the initiative group and the kindergarten teacher and helpers who did the intellectual work, not the visiting lecturers or Mercury agents. They discussed new forms of school management such as practiced in Waldorf schools (the College of Teachers) and such things as child-parent and child-teacher relationships; the attempt was made to create a strong sense of interdependence in spheres other than money. It was pointed out, for example, that one TV-watching child may affect his classmates, that group norms are necessary for children even if they can be oppressive for adult independence. No one quite forgot the question of financing a new building, but it was revived as a subject of discussion only when, after almost a year, several parents outside the initiative group wanted to talk about the future of their children, who would soon outgrow the kindergarten. The fact that none could benefit unless all participated became clear once again, but this time there was less holding back. The question of the Borrowing Community was re-evaluated, re-doubted, re-affirmed, and the initiative group was asked to approach Mercury once again to discuss it.

When the Mercury agents met with the whole parent group a second time, the central question was not "How are we going to pay for our building?" but "How can we best mobilize our resources in preparation for funding our school?" The ensuing discussion showed the results of the year's work in communication and consciousness-raising; the Mercury representatives did more listening than talking. There were questions, puzzlement, struggles, and contradictions, but the meeting showed an emerging community will, and in the end it was decided to establish a deposit account in Mercury in order to collect funds against the day when the school or the parents would have to borrow. A prospective Borrowing Community Treasury Group of three was appointed. The initiative group was asked to search for a building once again.

Four months later a new opportunity arose in the form of a nearby church school's closure. It was put on the market and the initiative group examined it. It was much cheaper—about £30,000—but would serve a growing school for only about four years, assuming a growth rate of one class per year. The parent body was apprised of the situation and with little delay expressed the will to go ahead. At the same time as finding the money, the school would have to find a teacher. The decision to move forward was on this occasion something that came from the wish of a majority of those concerned, not the determination—clearheaded though it might be—of a few. This wish was underpinned by two convictions: first, that Waldorf education would be important enough in the world and in their children's lives to make sacrifices for; and second, that the establishment of the school would have to be a group effort and would work only if each individual were prepared to sink his personal interests in the group interest. These two ideas had developed in the course of discussions during the previous year, but only at a cost: several parents had not shared these convictions and had placed their children in other schools. Other parents who came to the group during the year had not shared in the development of those ideas and did not find it easy to appreciate their importance. Rather they were aware of a slight cliquishness, even a sectarian mentality in the group. Clearly, finding a social balance that would permit freedom of thought alongside economic commitment was to be no easy task.

In the end, the cost of the building turned out to be more than £30,000, for inevitably there were a few repairs, the fees relating to the sale, and incidental expenses. The final figure was £34,000, which would include the first year's rates. Two of the new school's supporters were prepared to lend, unsecured and interest-free, £7,000 between them, but only for one year. Eighteen families formed the Borrowing Community. Each family's commitment would thus be £1,500 plus about 10% per annum interest. The loan was made for four years, so this meant that the family budget would include £9.00 per week beyond their share of the running costs of the school. Some families found this a serious burden and several of them clubbed together to undertake commercial fund-raising to meet their obligations: jewelry-making, secondhand book sales, pottery, and doll-making. They did not relieve only their own individual debts within the Borrowing Community but *one another's.* "Well," said one, "we're guaranteeing one another's debts in any case, and that's where the security for the loan lies. Working for one another is not all that difficult." At the same time several families who could afford to donate more contributed to the pooled repayments to ease the burden of those who found it a struggle.

Mercury and the Cathedral Waldorf School had one more task: to find the deposits that would provide the loan. We were confident that once a Borrowing Community had been set up, it would not be difficult to find people prepared to lend. And we were right: when we advertised the project it was soon 80% subscribed, and we already had deposits earmarked for Waldorf education in general, so a package could be made up with no difficulty. The important factor was that we could describe the solidarity of the parents as being the outstanding feature of the school, its strength and basis for its future.

Further Consequences:

The Cathedral Waldorf School did not have an easy life of it in the following two years. It had great difficulty in finding and keeping teachers, and several of the founding families had to move away from the district. Such stresses had little effect on the functioning of the Borrowing Community, however; in two cases the loans of departing members were taken over by new-comers and in the third case the departing member main-tained his repayments even though he was not going to benefit from the transaction.

The story has not yet finished, for the building purchased for the school had limitations, and when the school needs to move on or build an addition, it is clear that more money will have to be found. The Borrowing Community will have to grow and the support will have to be even stronger than before.

The two case histories just recounted are intended to demon-strate the necessity of community involvement in financing ini-tiatives. The Mercury Provident Society is no different from any bank in this respect. What is a bank, after all? It is, as far as loan money is concerned, a collecting point; depositors leave loan money in the hands of the banker so that he or she may decide where it should be invested. The banker is a representative of the communal financial will. The salient fact about Mercury's operation is that we try to make this as transparent and con-scious as we can. Thus the source point of money for lending is as far as possible the will of the depositor, not the decision of the banker; the source of the security is the will of guarantors, not the value of capital assets involved in the transaction.

The social value of an enterprise, not the material value of its equipment, is the expression of its real worth. The passage of money from lender to borrower via the bank is an expression of confidence and to some degree an agreement about spiritual and cultural values. Increasingly, people are aware that any initiative, positive or negative, needs financial blood if it is to become flesh.

In the case of Henry Smith such wider social consciousness was lacking. His problem would not be solved by a loan, and it is just as well that his motives and initiative were tested by the bankers whom he asked for finance. The refusal was possibly an important step in his self-knowledge, but on this very account the bankers bear some responsibility in the development of his destiny. In the case of the Cathedral Waldorf School, the people at the heart of the initiative knew that without a social context expressed as material support, their efforts would go for nought. If the deposits, direct loans, and guarantees were not forthcoming, then the social support would have proved itself to be no more than wishful thinking; there must be tests if an initiative wishes to show its strength. The bankers' role was catalytic; Mercury initiated the process of forming the Borrowing Community and provided the framework and financial harness for the initiative. These arrangements may have done much to determine the parent-school relationships for years to come: school and environment were interacting with one another via the medium of money flowing through the channel provided by the bank. The Borrowing Community enabled supporters to *donate* money to the infant initiative. Like parents or guardians, they undertook to clothe the school, with no benefit to themselves.

With a commercial initiative the relationship would be different. If Mercury were to lend, it would do so with the expectation that the initiative would be profitable, and if depositors shared this expectation, the loan would be made, and interest rates would be calculated as a balance between what the enterprise could afford and what the depositor would need as a return. Security would best be provided in the form of guarantees, and the best possible guarantors would be potential (or actual) customers.

Profitability raises the important question of legal structure and ownership of an undertaking. The most common forms today seem to be designed to reward successful investors (the limited company) or successful entrepreneurs (sole ownership or partnership). Cooperatively owned producer enterprises are rare, and those where profitability is completely separated from ownership are even rarer. Mercury encourages this latter structure as much as possible: one solution has been to form a limited company and issue its shares to a charity or multipurpose charitable trust whose function is twofold: first, to hold shares as a neutral guardian of the entrepreneur against hostile ownership; and second, to receive and distribute (or use) the profits in spiritual-cultural undertakings in need of gift money.

Throughout, the aim of Mercury in its financial dealings is to let investors' true intentions manifest themselves and to enable borrowers to see where their support comes from. The conventional bank manager's role hides depositor and borrower from one another. It is Mercury's intention to act as a sense organ so that each may perceive the other more clearly. A working community will find its financial support only if it has the organs that enable it to look and to see what is normally not visible.

4. Money in Initiatives—New Consciousness in Budgeting

Money circulates constantly through society, making visible an ever-moving "sea of values," and making possible an extraordinarily complex interdependence among human beings all over the world. Every new organization must find its place in this flow-pattern, and by doing so it will alter and contribute to the streams in which it stands. Managing the income and expenditures of an initiative means continually becoming conscious of the quality and quantity of money entering and leaving the organization, and making adjustments to achieve the appropriate balance in the specific situation. In this "conscious space" that an organization can create amid the flow of money through society, choices may be made and priorities established; between income and expenditure lies the possibility of human freedom asserting itself.

The threefold aspect of money described earlier finds its reflection also in the ongoing finances of a project. The qualities of *purchase money* and *gift money* have been characterized. In between lies a realm in which the transfer of funds is regulated by *contractual arrangements*, written or unwritten. Loans are a simple example of this; the "social contract" underlying taxation has also been mentioned. Contractual agreements assign rights and responsibilities to both parties; unlike gift or purchase, contract implies an ongoing relationship. *Purchase* is the exchange of what has been produced in the past; *gifts* make things possible for the *future: contracts* regulate the *present* state of relationship. This range of qualities of money will be perceptible in both the income and expenditure of most organizations. Identifying the particular configuration of sources of income and expenditure in one's own initiative, in terms of these three basic qualities, can become a fruitful starting point for penetrating the finances of an organization with consciousness, and taking them in hand as an integral part of the initiative process.

The following chart shows some examples of gift money, "contract money," and purchase money as they might appear as items in the revenue accounts of most organizations. Each institution will show its own specific configuration in this respect.

On the income side, we see money coming into the organization from one or a combination of three main sources— *sponsors, clients,* and *customers. Sponsors* are those institutions and individuals prepared to support the initiative financially without asking anything in return (gift). *Clients* will make payments to the organization in return for certain benefits, on an agreed *contractual* basis. *Customers* will pay a fixed *purchase price* for the goods or services produced.

	Income		Expenditure	
Given by *Sponsors*	Donations Voluntary subscriptions Grants, subsidies, etc.	"Gift" → Future	Surpluses donated (→future of society) Taxation (compulsory gift) Reinvestment, training + development (→future of organization) Distribution of profits	Given to *Beneficiaries*
Arranged with *Clients*	Fees: negotiated means-tested uniform scale of charges	"Contract" ↔ Present	Staff community Salaries Hired labor Pensions, etc.	Arranged between *Work-Partners*
Paid by *Customers*	Fixed prices for "packaged" services Sales of products	"Purchase" ← Past	Costs: e.g., Financial + professional services Transport, fuel, power Depreciation + maintenance Materials	Paid to *Suppliers*

On the expenditure side, we can see a reflection of these three kinds of relationships in the destination of the funds that flow out of an organization. Starting from the "purchase" aspect, we see first the true *costs* of an organization; much work must be done by others outside the organization before its own activity can take place. Those who do this work are the *suppliers* of the organization, and they must be paid. A further portion of expenditure must be used to meet the needs of those who work *within* the organization. There are many different bases for these arrangements, but whatever system is agreed upon, it will for the present constitute a formal or informal *contract* among the *work-partners* in the initiative. A third category of expenditure arises when not all available funds are absorbed by the first two categories. The creation of surpluses or profits may be a major aim of the organization, or may arise incidentally; if surpluses do not occur in any form, absence of such funds may lead to severe restrictions on the development of the organization and the people within it. Surpluses may be given away internally or externally; internal "gifts" would include new investment within the organization, as well as the provision of training and self-development facilities for staff, and the distribution of profits among employees and/or shareholders. In the case of profit-making organizations, the state will take a portion of any financial surplus in taxation, which is a kind of "compulsory gift" needed to fund those facilities that the state then provides "free" for its citizens. Surpluses can, of course, also be freely and creatively gifted, through a trust or similar body, to meet human needs in any chosen social or cultural field. The "gift" is thus a contribution toward the future of one's own organization and/or of the wider society: those who receive this gift money, directly or indirectly, are the *beneficiaries* of the initiative.

EXERCISE
Budgeting

Financial planning in an initiative means lifting oneself out of the flow of day-to-day transactions, into the abstraction of figures, in order to become more consciously able to perceive and guide the economic consequences of one's activities. Often this process gives rise to explicit or implicit policy decisions, and these may or may not correspond to the overall direction agreed upon in other discussions. Sometimes people start to wonder: Are we in control of our project and its finances, or are the finances controlling us?

In such situations the following exercise can be helpful. First, try to set out the project's finances for a recent period, with figures, in the "threefold" form shown on page 152. Place items in the different areas according to how you see the services of part-time employees as a cost, like the electricity bill, or are these people part of a "social contract" arrangement that includes human considerations? There will, of course, be grey areas, but this "placing" of items (income as well as expenditure) can already reveal much about the attitudes underlying financial policy.

This can be made more explicit by working with the following questions:

Income:

1. What are our products? Are they still attractive in quality and price? Are we still in touch with our market's requirements? What are realistic targets for sales income?

2. Who are our clients? Are the agreements we have with them still mutually satisfactory, or do some things need renegotiating? In what ways do we aim to deepen or broaden these relationships, and what effect will this have on our income?

3. Who are our sponsors? What aspects of our activity are people most willing to support with gifts? How can we develop this support, and what financial expression of it can be expected?

> *Expenditure:*
>
> 1. Which of our costs are fixed, i.e., related to time, and which are variable, i.e., related to our actual activity? What "standard of living"—physical environment, facilities, salaries—does our initiative need? Does our spending pattern reflect our true priorities in this realm?
>
> 2. On what basis do we support our staff, ourselves, each other? Do these arrangements correspond to the relation we want to have among ourselves? What are our guiding values in distributing resources to individuals?
>
> 3. Who are the beneficiaries of our enterprise? What are our development aims—for them, for ourselves, for the project? What investment in physical and/or human resources will be required?

Handling Purchase Money

This is the most apparently "objective" use of money—in straightforward buying and selling, people can feel on firm ground. Budgeting can and should be accurate here, both of income and expenditure. Those responsible will ask themselves questions such as:

- If a higher quality product is more expensive, what level of quality and cost is truly appropriate to the needs of our customers?
- What level is appropriate in supplying our own organization?
- Production and consumption use up resources, some scarce: what is our responsibility to the Earth and our fellow humans in what we use and what we waste?
- Do we wish to charge the maximum price for our products (market forces) or can we, perhaps in dialogue with clients, work toward a concept of "true price," i.e., what we need to receive in order to continue producing on a satisfactory basis?

The purchase principle, perhaps because most accessible and transparent, often tends to spill over into realms where it is not appropriate and produces distortions; thus we speak, for instance, of a "labor market," and even a "money market" as if labor and capital were commodities to be bought and sold, like carrots. Purchase money tries to present all transactions as purchases, often thereby obscuring their true nature. For example, a pension fund is a set of contractual agreements whereby those at work now support those who have retired. Provided the fund continues, they can expect to be supported themselves later. In reality there are rights and responsibilities involved here, but no commodities; yet we often think of "buying into" such a scheme, in purchase terms—and advertising may present it as a "good bargain." In managing the finances of an initiative then, it will be important to distinguish the true *costs* of the operation (that is, the cost of commodities purchased from outside) from contractual arrangements, made internally or externally. This distinction, by reasserting the freedom of people to negotiate the financial relationships they want, can diffuse much of the power and powerlessness often experienced in relation to money.

Handling Contractual Money

Contractual money is created and moved as a result of *agreements* worked out between people. These sometimes take the form of an apparent exchange (for example, so much money for so much work) and sometimes tend more to the "gift" element (for example, a deed of covenant). Typically, contractual money expresses a *state of relationship* between the parties involved. *The intention to create and maintain a certain type of relationship* is the guiding principle here.

For instance, an institution providing educational or therapeutic facilities to its clients may wish simply to sell those services on a semi-commercial basis (for example, a private language or secretarial school), in which case the appropriate form will be a fixed "price" for a certain course of lessons or treatment. However, an increased sense of responsibility to clients may lead to the granting of scholarships or reductions for those less able to pay, such as the elderly or unemployed. This "sliding scale" of fees may be means-tested or even individually negotiated. Here, a quite different principle from that of sale and purchase becomes visible. When, from the other side, the responsibility of clients and supporters increases in the same way, one may see "contracts" such as voluntary subscriptions or regular contributions entered into, which are more akin to gifts.

Many voluntary and political organizations work in this way; a charitable trust may have a nominal subscription fee conferring certain rights and privileges on its members, while also relying heavily on donations. A campaign organization may give some guidelines to its supporters that take account of personal circumstances—waged / unwaged family, and so on. An independent school that wishes to move away from the "selling" of education may ask for a percentage of family income from those who send their children to the school.

A similar spectrum of alternative arrangements can be seen *within* an organization, in the way in which financial support is provided for its staff. It is usual in our society to base remuneration for work on a person's capacities, for example, skills, seniority, level of responsibility, but some newer social initiatives are trying to move away from this "purchase of capacities" toward an increased mutual responsibility in providing for each other's needs. Such projects will tend to assume a high level of non-financial motivation among staff, which "releases" funds from the incentive function, so that money can be used more effectively to meet human needs. It is in principle quite uneconomic to have to "bribe" people into working hard!

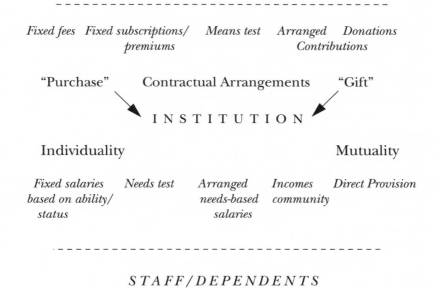

CLIENTS / SPONSORS

- -

Fixed fees   *Fixed subscriptions/*   *Means test*   *Arranged*   *Donations*
premiums   *Contributions*

"Purchase"   Contractual Arrangements   "Gift"

I N S T I T U T I O N

Individuality   Mutuality

Fixed salaries   *Needs test*   *Arranged*   *Incomes*   *Direct Provision*
based on ability/   *needs-based*   *community*
status   *salaries*

- -

STAFF/DEPENDENTS

In commercial organizations, the concept of "added value" can be a helpful starting point from which to move away from the image of labor as a *cost*. In simple terms, added value can be defined as the difference between the total income of a firm from sales, and the cost of goods and services supplied from outside. This difference is the value added by the work of those in the organization who use its capital facilities.

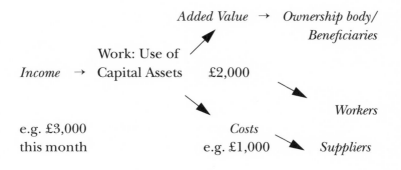

Added Value → *Ownership body/*
Beneficiaries

Work: Use of
Income → Capital Assets   £2,000

Workers

e.g. £3,000   *Costs*
this month   e.g. £1,000   *Suppliers*

The added value thus generated can then be divided on any agreed contractual basis among the staff of the firm, with a portion allocated to the trustees or owners of the capital assets for development and other "gift" purposes. This "contractual sharing of added value," which has been adopted, for example, by a printing cooperative that we know of, effectively overcomes the indignity and alienation experienced, often unconsciously, by those whose work is treated as a commodity. In noncommercial projects, the amounts available to support staff will relate to the *recognition* that their activity receives from wider society, rather than the creation of added value, but internally there will be similar decisions to be made regarding the criteria for distribution.

These criteria may combine elements of "need," seniority, level of skill, and responsibility, in any chosen form. A small woodworking firm, for instance, whose salary structure has grown rather haphazardly, has recently started experimenting with the use of three main criteria—skill, responsibility, and need. Within each of these, different levels have been identified that can be immediately recognized and related to—in this way the workers can find their own place and basis for remuneration in the firm. Something like the following table emerges:

CRITERION	LEVELS		
SKILL	Apprentice	Journeyman	Master
RESPONSIBILITY	For own work only	For a department or aspect	For the totality of a firm
NEED	Single person	Post-family	Family to support

"Needs-based" arrangements may take the form of individually agreed-upon salaries, of incomes communities whose members draw from a common pool of money, or of residential communities where most needs are directly provided for the coworkers of the institution. One danger with "needs-based" systems can be that "needs" quickly become interpreted as "subsistence level," and the idealism of the coworkers is exploited (often by themselves!) to conceal the fact that the project is basically underfinanced. Unless people are substantially freed from moral pressure in determining their own needs, such arrangements can be experienced as a straitjacket rather than a liberation. The aim here must be to find the appropriate outer arrangements to express and sustain the actual relationship that the staff want (and are *able*) to have to each other and to their organization. The "purchase" end of this spectrum emphasizes *self-responsibility*; the separation of remuneration from individual performance emphasizes *mutual responsibility*. Each project must find its own way of balancing these two principles.

Accurate budgeting for contractual finance is perfectly possible, at least in the short- and medium-term, as soon as the chosen arrangements are agreed upon and clear. They must also be specific. For instance, to state that: "Staff can draw money to meet their private needs from our current account," may quickly become chaotic unless it is translated into a definite arrangement such as: "Any two of three mandated members may sign checks on the current account to meet staff needs, up to a maximum of £35,000 per annum. Not more than £4,000 may be drawn in any single month. The resulting financial picture will be reviewed quarterly in the staff meeting."

A group of teachers we worked with decided to set up a community bank account, into which a lump sum would be paid each term by the school where it worked. The teachers would each have a "cash card" with which to draw from this account, and meet regularly to share their assessments of their own needs, make informal agreements as to the amount each would draw in a given period, and formulate their joint request to the school for the following term. In this way, the individual aspect of staff finance was placed entirely in the hands of those directly affected—only the total amount required became the concern of the school Council responsible for approving the overall budget. In general, this arrangement works well—it is experienced not as *easier*, but as more "real" than a conventional salary system.

On this basis, contractual finance can be handled both humanly and accurately. This would also apply, for example, to the terms of a private loan, or undertakings from a support or client group to provide income for the project. Reliability in budgeting rests not on the market, as with purchase money, but on mutual trust and responsibility among staff, clients, and supporters.

Handling Gift Money

We generally think of "gifts" in terms of small-scale altruism—coins in a charity collecting box, or Christmas presents for family and friends. But in fact all money that is used to meet social or cultural requirements, without demanding anything economically in return, is moving according to the "gift" principle. Funding for education, medicine, the arts, religion, welfare benefits—this money is all "given": the values it represents are not immediately needed to support economic producers. In many cases the responsibility for the gifting process is taken over by the state, which uses income from taxation (compulsory gifts) to support, and also control, certain cultural and social activities. Such state-controlled gifts can become an anonymous, bureaucratic, and even oppressive system.

Many small-scale initiatives, however, will have the opportunity and the need to handle gift money that is made available by relatively free human decisions, especially in cases where state sponsorship is not available. Gifts will need to be attracted both for the establishment of capital assets and for some proportion of ongoing revenue. A key aspect here is *communication*. Gift funding can flow freely when needs are made visible in the right way, in the right place, and when an appropriate social framework is seen to be available to receive and use it. An appeal for gifts must touch the *inner* needs and impulses of the sponsor, not his outer requirements as in the case of a purchase. It must therefore express in imaginative form the inner aims and values of the project seeking support, and communicate these "heart to heart."

Self-examination is therefore the first step toward finding gift money. Do we have the energy and commitment to communicate our vision so that others can become enthused by it? Are our aims clear and important enough—not only to ourselves!—to attract the support needed? Can we kindle a real social warmth around the project? Are our proposed activities really wanted by others?

Secondly, in seeking gift finance, it can often be helpful to "think backward" by imagining oneself in a situation where the required funds *had* been made available: where would they have come from? Every individual and organization not engaged in economic production is in fact supported by an invisible network of conscious and/or unconscious sponsors: in actively seeking gift funding, one needs to make this actual and potential web of connections visible to oneself. Try to form as vivid and full a picture as possible of one's past, present, and possible future connections in this respect. Can one imagine certain specific sources of gifts, providing the required amount over the required period? For example, a student seeking sponsors for a year's course might imagine a small grant from one of three foundations known to have supported previous students on the same course, plus a few pounds a week from, say, six out of ten friends or relatives who could be approached. If a number of different combinations can be imagined to find the funds needed, the person will have increased chances of success. In many cases the personal connections of those involved will be as decisive as the worthiness of their aims.

FUNDAMENTAL SOCIAL LAW

In a community of human beings working together the well-being of the community will be greater, the less an individual claims the proceeds of his or her own work, i.e., the more of these proceeds one makes over to others and the more one's own requirements are satisfied not out of one's own work, but out of the work done by others.

• Every institution in a community of human beings that is contrary to this law will inevitably engender in some part of it, after a while, suffering and want.

• It is a fundamental law that holds good for all social life with the same absoluteness and necessity as any law of nature within a particular field of natural causation.

• It must not be supposed, however, that it is sufficient to acknowledge this law as one for general moral conduct, or to try and interpret it into the sentiment that everyone should work for the good of others.

• This law only finds its living, fitting expression in actual reality when a community of human beings succeeds in creating institutions of such a kind that no one can ever claim the results of one's own labor for one's self, but that they all, to the last fraction, go wholly to the benefit of the community.

And the individual, again, must be supported in return by the labor of others. The important point is, therefore, that working for others and the object of obtaining so much income must be kept apart as two separate things.

Extracted from: *Anthroposophy and the Social Question*, Rudolf Steiner 1905/1906.

The third step will be to assess these imaginative pictures. Are they realistic? If not, certain expectations may have to be adjusted. It is vital to eliminate wishful thinking at this stage, to move from: "If only someone would give us $x. . . ." to "If these people give what we can reasonably ask of them. . . ." If realism is achieved, than the fourth step of approaching potential sponsors becomes a kind of active research into one's own and the project's destiny. If the aims and needs of the initiative are communicated without sentimentality or manipulation, then one can receive gifts without incurring moral obligations.

The truly free gift is a rare thing in our society. In many cases the gifting process is mediated and determined by a political process; in many others, an apparent gift is in fact a concealed form of purchase, as in much commercial "sponsorship" of sport, and so on. Organizations that are in a position to generate or mediate the flow of gift money can in this realm directly create freedom for others. In order to fulfil this potential, they will need to act scrupulously both in the exercise of their own decision-making responsibilities, and in resisting the temptation to extend the responsibility beyond the moment when the gift is made by attaching strings or conditions.

Social and cultural initiatives and their supporters have an important task for the future in creating forms and procedures whereby the flow of gift money to support what is seen to be needed becomes an *objective process* alongside the spontaneous expression of generosity. When this process happens, reliable budgeting will be possible in this realm also, and the "faith" on which it is based will not be "blind faith," but an objective faith in the spiritual impulses underlying human decisions.

5. Sense-Organs for Money

Money has a direct connection to the human Ego. It affects us in ways that can be intimidating, paralyzing, fascinating, fructifying. It tests our courage and integrity. It must serve our initiatives but often appears or attempts to control them. It facilitates our organizational and individual lives but may, if we allow it, take on a life of its own. Its potential for social harm can be overcome only by conscious mutual support between human beings.

We have spoken of the bank as a "sense-organ," and the need for initiatives to develop organs for "what is not normally visible." We have also tried to show that one can develop a sense for the different qualities that money can take on. In moving from purchase money through contractual money to gift money, the sense-organs required become progressively more inward. Our judgements regarding *purchase money* can be based on market research, on evaluation of products, and on dialogue with customers and suppliers. A sense for the appropriate arrangements in *contractual finance* can only be gained through discussions with a background of mutual trust, interest, and knowledge. In seeking *gift finance,* we need to conduct a vigorous research into our own motivation and destiny. In these ways the power of money can be harnessed toward the fulfillment of our social and spiritual aims.[7]

---

7. Also see the four booklets edited by John Cellier, *The Economic Basis for Waldorf Education*—Volume 1, *The Nature of Money,* Threefold Educational Foundation, 285 Hungry Hollow Road, Spring Valley, NY 10977.

7

Re-creating the Organization
Vision, Mission, and Long-Range Planning

CHRISTOPHER SCHAEFER

The creative mind exceeds this liberty in being able to redefine itself and reality at large, generating whole new sets of
alternatives.... In this sense we call creative vision the edge of
freedom, the evolutionary faculty by which down through history we have redefined our world and ourselves.

Robert Grudin[1]

Why Do Visioning and Long-Range Planning?

For any organization engaging in a long-range planning process is a strenuous effort. It is an extra, in addition to the daily
and weekly work of running the school, the clinic, or the store.
Yet it is also a source of renewal, like an occasional retreat for
the individual; an opportunity to reflect on the past biography
of the initiative, assess present strengths and weaknesses, and
create a commonly willed image and plan for the future.

Such a process is most appropriate in times of transition for
the organization: facing a major move, entering into a new
phase of development, embarking on a capital campaign, or
facing a transition of leadership. It is in such times that a conscious and shared look at past, present, and future is needed to

---

1. See Robert Grudin, *The Grace of Great Things, Creativity and Innovation* (NY:
Tickur and Fields, 1990), for the lead quote and wonderful reflections on
the creative process.

provide a common focus for our commitment. Typical examples of such transitions that I have worked with include:

- a very successful community college in the crisis of the pioneer phase;
- a company in the papermaking supplier industry in which new technology was changing the industry;
- a small research organization that had suddenly become quite successful and needed to look at options for the future;
- a large alternative adult education center that needed to engage and deepen the commitment of its staff;
- a spiritual movement that was in danger of becoming market driven;
- a Waldorf school that was exploring the question of starting a high school.

Visioning and Planning as Re-creating
the Organization and Community Building

A long-range planning process involves understanding the past: the initiative's biography, history, and patterns of development; assessing present strengths and weaknesses, and imagining the future. This understanding of the past, evaluating the present, and imagining the future is really a re-creation of the organization in the consciousness of all those participating in the long-range planning process. Such re-creation is an act of freedom. The redefinition and re-creation of our institutional world and ourselves within it is the central component of visioning and long-range planning. It is that activity through which we can most consciously experience ourselves as creators and co-creators of our social world. Our experience of this re-creation at an individual and collective level is usually direct and can be quite powerful. For example, as we hear the biography of the institution and add our experience to it, we are raising to consciousness the story, the myth of the institution and our role within it. Such a biography is an epos, a heroic story in which everyone has contributed in his or her own way. As we then think and imagine the school or the therapy center's future and are listened to by others, we are sharing our hopes and dreams for the institution and for ourselves.

The type of long-range planning process we are describing is comprehensive, systematic, and, above all, inclusive. If it is a school, then faculty, parents, staff, and board need to be involved in some meaningful way. A visioning and long-range planning process is a community-building dialogue in which all those connected to the institution can have the opportunity to express and align their intentions with a common imagination of the future. The process of discussion and involvement is as important as the result, for without achieving a commonality of vision the organization cannot move forward.

The following conditions are important in entering a long-range planning process.

1. A shared sense that now is the right time to engage in long-range planning. If the organization is in major financial crisis or extensive conflict, or if it has recently gone through a planning process, then clearly a new planning process is not appropriate. This is also true for new initiatives in which intuition, enthusiasm, and flexibility are most important—not an extensive planning process. The right time is when the institution faces a major transition in its life and when people sense a need for dialogue, renewal, and commitment.

2. The recognition that long-range planning is an extra. Typically a comprehensive and inclusive process will take from six months to a year and require a number

of retreats and meetings. I would say it should not extend for more than a year, for if it does, it can become the focus of discontent (why so long? not another meeting? on a beautiful May weekend? and so on).

3. The process needs to be supported and carried by the Leadership Group.

4. The planning process needs to be systematic and sequential. The length of the process, the steps and activities, and the level of involvement of different individuals and groups should be clearly articulated.

5. The planning process needs to be seen as a community-building process.

6. There should be a recognition that the long-term planning process will bring about changes in the organization and in people. A successful planning process is a clarification of perception and values. Again and again I have experienced individuals going through such a process who say, "I cannot stay here" or "Now I am finally able to commit myself." Long-term planning will inevitably bring to the surface hidden areas of agreement and disagreement and bring with it discomfort as well as enthusiasm.

7. Long-term planning is a dialogue with the gods. Such a statement could be easily misunderstood; what I mean has three components. The first is that unfolding events have an uncanny ability to obstruct or change our best laid plans. We need to expect such changes; there is a deeper reality than we are necessarily aware of in both our individual lives and in our institution's development. Knowing this, we can observe how the institution and the world respond to our vision and plan and then make inner and outer adjustments.

The second relates to an image from ancient times. In many religious practices, priests offered incense or some other sacrifice in order to converse with the gods. The offering was the beginning of the dialogue. In this sense I see a vision and a long-term plan as an offering to the spirit of the organization.

Throughout the planning process we can have the sense that we are in a dialogue with people and also conversing with the spirit. A further part of this awareness is that listening is as important as speaking. Can we so listen to each other and to the spiritual world during this process that the gods begin to speak to us?

As Brenda Uland has noted, "When we are listened to, it creates us, makes us unfold and expand. Ideas actually begin to grow within us and come to life."[2] Does the spirit of the organization need to be listened to with such attention? If it is, I believe the vision, mission, and long-term plan can become a true expression of the identity of the being of the organization.

8. The long-term planning process needs to be reviewed and the plan itself updated periodically.

Steps in a Long-Range Planning Process

When organizations consider beginning a long-range planning process there is often little clarity about what is involved or of the different steps and qualities needed. In the following description I will outline some of the steps, qualities, and distinctions that I found to be helpful in working on long-range planning with a variety of groups and organizations. They are offered in the spirit of describing possibilities, not rules, since each institution will need to define its own process.

---

2. Brenda Uland, "Tell Me More, on the Fine Art of Listening," *Utne Reader* (November/December, 1992).

I. PREPARATION

While it may be tempting to think that we can fashion a new self or a new organization by planning, to do so is clearly not possible. An understanding of the organization's history and of its present strengths and weaknesses is therefore an essential foundation.

1. Biographical Review:

- When was the college, company, clinic, school, or store started?
- By whom was it started?
- What was the first set of critical questions?
- What has been the historical development?
- What are the themes, patterns, and relationships in the initiative's biography?

For example, the Association for Research and Enlightenment (A.R.E.), in Virginia Beach, has been led and guided by three generations of Cayces, first Edgar Cayce, then Hugh Lynn Cayce, and then Charles Thomas Cayce, each giving a particular stamp to the organization. The New York Open Center was based on a close working relationship between Ralph White, an experienced program person, and a New York lawyer, Walter Beebe, whose vision, drive, connections, and administrative capacities helped this initiative get off the ground. The Asten group, in the paper-forming fabric business, has, through generations, been guided by a partnership between a sales personality and a technical engineering person. In each case these personalities and relationships have played an important role in the institution's history.

The biography needs to be more than a superficial narrative, and people need to be given the opportunity to comment and to contribute. However, it is often best to give an individual or a small group the task to pull this together in draft form.

2. Assessment of Current Strengths and Weaknesses:

- What are the present strengths and weaknesses of the school, store, clinic, association, or company?
- How well is it organized?
- What are its finances like?
- What are the present organizational forms? Which work and which don't?
- What about the quality of relationships between people within the organization and also with customers, clients, or parents?
- What phase of development is the organization in?
- How is the dialogue with the spirit, with people, and with the earth?
- What issues would coworkers and clients like to see addressed?

In doing such a self-assessment, it is often good to prepare a questionnaire for people both outside and within the organization, following up with selected interviews. A review and sharing can then take place in a conference with coworkers and others.

3. Assumptions about the Future

As an additional part of the preparation it is important to make some assumptions about the future—about the kind of development that will affect the environment of the organization. Will the town and the community still need a private school? What are the population and income projections for the county? Will the future bring a still greater interest in natural foods and alternative medicine? This last question is critical for the health food industry and for alternative approaches to healing. For each initiative there are a number of quite specific questions the answers to which will affect its future directly and some more general assumptions that will need to be discussed. While some research will help, often we need to make educated guesses about the likely interest in our service or product and about the probable evolution of the economy.

Having completed these steps, the organization can enter planning for the future with a shared sense of identity. Without such a basis, planning can become an illusion.

In the following diagram some of the further steps in the long-term planning process are described.

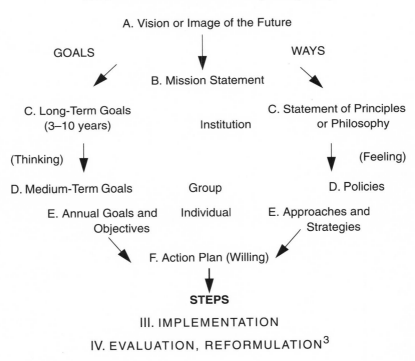

I. PREPARATION
1. Biography
2. Strengths and Weaknesses
3. Assumptions about the Future

II. LONG-TERM PLANNING (0–20 years)

A. Vision or Image of the Future

GOALS   WAYS

B. Mission Statement

C. Long-Term Goals   Institution   C. Statement of Principles
(3–10 years)   or Philosophy

(Thinking)   (Feeling)

D. Medium-Term Goals   Group   D. Policies

E. Annual Goals and   Individual   E. Approaches and
Objectives   Strategies

F. Action Plan (Willing)

STEPS

III. IMPLEMENTATION

IV. EVALUATION, REFORMULATION[3]

3. I am indebted to W.J. Hasper and F. Glasl, *Von Kooperativer Markstrategie zur Unternehmungs-entwicklung,* (Bern: Paul Haupt, 1988) for some of these ideas on the planning process.

The diagram presents two different dimensions to the planning—on the right those activities that represent the values and principles of the organization that reflect more the feeling life, and on the left the more analytical, rational goal-setting activities.

II. LONG-TERM PLANNING

A. *Vision or Image of the Future*

A vision of the future is an imagination of what we would like the organization to be ten to twenty years from now. It needs to contain a dream that can motivate and guide, like a star that gives light to navigate by. This is not an easy thing to develop, for it is not a question of describing more buildings, students, or products but rather a combination of qualities and activities that form a living whole.

The Door, a New York center for adolescents, had a vision of a totally integrated set of services for young people in need: counseling, nutrition, an alternative high school, job training, athletic and exercise programs, and a referral service all in one location. When the New York Open Center started, it had a vision of being a center for spirituality, embracing both Eastern and Western esoteric traditions in downtown Manhattan. Henry Ford had a vision of designing and producing an automobile so efficiently and paying such good wages that everyone could afford a Model T. A vision, if it addresses a real need in the world, has a way of drawing around it the people and resources needed to make it happen.

B. *The Mission Statement*

As Peter Drucker pointed out in his book *Managing the Non-Profit Organization*, "A mission statement has to focus on what the institution really tries to do."[4] It should not be too long or too complicated, and it should have implications for the operation of the organization. Waldorf schools often state that their mission is to educate for freedom. This then needs some elaboration so that the teachers, parents, and friends know what is meant and know what their contribution to the mission can be. The A.R.E., the spiritual movement founded by Edgar Cayce, has the mission of making manifest the love of God and man through Awakening, Educating, Applying, Sharing, and Serving.[5] The mission of the New York Open Center is to be "a focal point for holistic thinking and practice in the heart of New York City."[6] Sears Roebuck used to have the mission of being the informed and responsible buyer for the American family, which was an incredibly successful approach to retailing until a few years ago. A consultancy group of which I am part has the mission of helping individuals, groups, and institutions take their next steps in development.

There are a number of important factors regarding the mission of an organization:

- Keeping it simple
- Doing what you already do better
- Really making a difference—responding to a real need
- Believing in what you are doing
- Trying to make it live in all of your activity

C. A Statement of Philosophy or Principles

If we now return to the diagram on long-term planning, two paths are indicated, a path of goals and another of ways or

---

4. Peter Drucker, *Managing the Non-Profit Organization, Principles and Practices* (NY: Harper, Collins, 1990).
5. A.R.E. Long-Range Plan, 1986.
6. New York Open Center—Mission Statement-draft, 1990.

means. I have usually preferred to move from the mission statement to a statement of philosophy or values, as the mission quite naturally leads to these kinds of reflections. The W. K. Kellogg Foundation has a philosophical commitment to life-long open learning, supporting the education of its employees.[7] Mabou, a successful small department store in Saratoga Springs, New York, had a philosophy of treating the customer as a guest and the salesperson as a host. It also worked at allowing each employee to become what they were capable of being. The Asten Group, a forming-fabric manufacturer for the paper industry, has the philosophy of creating a true sense of community in the company.

Statements of principles should also include statements about how the organization is structured and the quality of relationships.

D. A Statement of Long-Term Goals (3-10 years)

The statement of long-term goals needs to articulate the major goals of the organization over a longer period of time, anywhere from three to ten years. In their last long-term plan (1980-90) the A.R.E. had the goal of becoming a major publisher and distributor of quality books related to psychic research and of increasing their membership sevenfold. The goals of the Shining Mountain Waldorf School in Boulder, Colorado, included starting a high school and building an arts complex and auditorium. The New York Open Center had goals of building an active board and a number of larger courses and programs connected to professional training.

A statement of long-term goals should not be too complex and should contain clear priorities.

---

7. W. K. Kellogg Foundation, *This We Believe*.

The Principals of a Successful Business—MABOU
by Mark Strauss

For over eighteen years Mabou has successfully marketed its unique blend of products by following its own special philosophy. These are some of the principals that we have relied upon:

The buying and selling of goods is a secondary function, we are a service organization serving the needs of the community. We are an integral part of the quality of life in Saratoga Springs. Sales volume is related to how well we service the needs of our local, regional, and visiting population.

Treat the customer as a human being. Being honest with a customer often means convincing them not to buy something—but that honesty will always bring them back.

Do not think in terms of salespeople and customers—we are the hosts and they are the guests. Real service is not just a list of available conveniences, but rather an intuitive understanding of what someone needs. For one person it might be gift wrapping, for another a public restroom, still another might need help down the stairs and out to their car. A free shopping bag even though nothing was bought, an expert opinion on fashion, direction to SPAC or sometimes just a friendly smile. Always speak to the individual, not to the masses. The success of our marketing approach has been our attempt to reach people on a one-to-one basis. Our mailing list of over 10,000 current customers is sorted by people's interests. The most effective messages are those that appeal to these interests. Our newsletters have always been personal letters about personalities and specific areas of interest.

Allow each employee to become the most they are capable of becoming. Hiring good people, training well, and paying well are not enough. Most people are looking for personal satisfaction in what they do and the best way to satisfy that is to encourage creativity. Allowing people to develop their abilities in marketing, buying, and management requires more effort on the part of managers but results in a more motivated staff.

When times get tough—do the opposite of what everyone else is doing. Over the years Mabou has constantly responded to slowdowns in the business cycle by increasing inventory, giving across-the-board pay increases, and increasing the level of customer service. The message this sends to employees and customers is that they are not going to be sacrificed. Employees tend to work even harder to pull in new sales when they realize the company has their concerns in mind.

E. Medium-Term Goals, Approaches, and Policies

Medium-term goals should consist of a breakdown of major goals into distinct areas and contain statements about how these goals are to be achieved. These "how" statements reflect strategies and values, and an assessment of what activities are likely to be most successful in achieving the desired goals within the value framework of the organization. They can include extending the range of products or services, raising salaries, or improving profitability. Goal areas and policies naturally extend the mission statement and philosophy of the institution. In the case of a high school, policies about teacher hiring, financial aid, discipline, or salaries indicate how the institution will carry out its day-to-day activities within the context of preferred values. For companies, policies on quality, assessment, customer relations, and decision-making have the same impact. If policies are not articulated and do not reflect the statement of principles or philosophy of the organization then that philosophy becomes an unread Bible sitting in the lowest desk drawer of a few individuals.

F. Annual Goals, Objectives, Approaches, and the Action Plan

Annual goals, objectives, and approaches describe what you hope to achieve in the next year or two. If the New York Open Center wants to extend the range of longer courses and seminars, how many of these and in what areas in year 1,2,3,4? If the Community Supported Agriculture project has the long-range goal of hiring two gardeners and having 250 supporting families then what has to be achieved in year 1, in year 2, and how? If Sunbridge College wishes to become a University of the Spirit, what kind of programs and activities are needed to help it move from being predominately a teacher training center?

The articulation of annual goals, objectives, and approaches already describes much of the action plan, which then spells out who will do what and how results will be reviewed.

III. THE PLANNING PROCESS AND THE IMPLEMENTATION OF THE LONG-RANGE PLAN

Before turning to the question of implementation I want to refer to a number of essential factors that affect the success or failure of the planning process and the plan itself.

The planning process should not take too long, or the organization will experience it as an excessive burden. In my experience it should not take longer than a year. In addition the process needs to be carried as a high priority by the key individuals or leadership group of the organization. If it is not carried as a high priority it is experienced as hollow or as a diversion by the rest of the organization. A connected issue is the degree to which the leadership group and the organization as a whole model, believe in, and attempt to embody the values and priorities expressed in the plan. The phrase "to walk the talk" contains wisdom. Lastly, and I think extremely important, is the degree to which the whole organization shares the vision, mission, and plan. The more it is owned, the greater the chance of success. Therefore the process of participation and involvement is as important as the documents produced. Opportunities for involvement, comment, and discussion should be given to all members of the organizational family—including support staff. How this is done depends on the size and nature of the organization.[8]

The question of implementation is dependent upon whether the plan is fully integrated as an ongoing basis into the life of the institution as opposed to being carried only by a small planning group with limited authority. Is it reviewed regularly by the board and the main decision-making groups? Is it integrated into the discussion and decisions of committees or departments?

---

8. I am indebted to Professor Mark Kriger of the School of Business, University of New York, for his research on organizational vision.

IV. EVALUATION AND REFORMULATION

For the long-term plan to have meaning it must contain goals and activities that are capable of being reviewed. Did we achieve what we wanted in the area of services, programs, and finances and in the time anticipated? If not, were we unrealistic to begin with, did we set the wrong priorities or not free enough people to work on them? If the plan is for five years or even three, then a quarterly review of activities and progress needs to be done and periodic adjustments made in goals and timetable.

As a plan only has validity for a limited period of time—between three to ten years—and as organizations and people change, a new planning process will be periodically needed to renew the focus and commitment of the initiative to re-create and redirect the organization.

Hygiene of the Organizational Soul:
A Consensus Vision Process That Generates Enthusiasm and Commitment

by Jean Yeager —August 1993

The Case: The Baltimore Waldorf School
Several purposes were clearly articulated by the president and vice-president of the board and by the faculty chair:

1. The school had recently been restructured by a joint faculty/board/parent committee. The recent past had been stressful for the school community. It was felt that it was important to "reconnect" as a community.

2. There were pressures for change in many places: location and site constraints; a high school program was being discussed; creating multicultural programs and programs for children with "special needs" were requested; and many more "issues" had been discussed and debated. There were multiple "visions" for the future being formed. The board and faculty felt the need to reach a "consensus" about the priorities for the future. Originally it was thought that by the end of this meeting everyone should have "action plans"—later it was agreed that this would have been too ambitious.

DESCRIPTION OF THE VISION MEETING PROCESS

Pre-Meeting Data Collection
A four-question survey was distributed to all the parents, teachers, and staff of the school (a total of about 90). Approximately 20 of these were returned before the Friday evening meeting. Answers to each question were written up verbatim on flip-chart pages and taped to the walls. All responses were collated by questions and written together. Also, responses (some quite critical) to a capital campaign survey that had been recently taken up were also put on the wall.

Friday Evening
Friday evening approximately 50 teachers, parents, and friends of the school gathered in the school multipurpose room. As they arrived, many went to the walls to see what was written on the sheets—there they found their own verbatim responses to the questionnaires among the responses of the others.

The purpose of the evening was to introduce the vision weekend agenda and reflect back on the history of the school. One teacher who was among the first to join the school recalled moments from the school's past. She recalled a moment when the real "vision" became something definite. An experienced Waldorf teacher had moved from an established school to join their effort. Her dedication to the young children and this school's effort was an inspiration that helped deepen the teacher's commitment and connection with Waldorf education. Her commitment helped as a catalyst that caused the teachers at that time to say, "yes we are a Waldorf school" and to move away from the community that had nourished the school to that point.

Following these "biographical" remarks, the chairperson of the board recalled the recent past to present history of the last year. He detailed the situation of the past year, town meetings, restructuring, financial condition, etc., and reported where the school stands today.

Homework for the evening was for those coming back to remember: "What inspired them to connect their destiny/lives with this school?"

Saturday
Saturday begins in a light, social fashion with singing. Following this, the agenda for the visioning process followed this path:

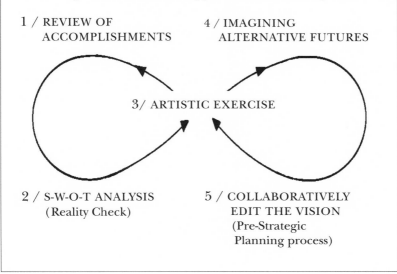

1 / REVIEW OF
     ACCOMPLISHMENTS

4 / IMAGINING
     ALTERNATIVE FUTURES

3/ ARTISTIC EXERCISE

2 / S-W-O-T ANALYSIS
   (Reality Check)

5 / COLLABORATIVELY
    EDIT THE VISION
    (Pre-Strategic
    Planning process)

Lemniscate Step1/Review of Accomplishments
In small groups participants listed three or four of the most significant accomplishments the school had made in the recent past. A scribe for each group collected answers, writing them on flip charts without editing. These were reported in plenum.

Coffee Break

Lemniscate Step 2/S-W-O-T Analysis
In plenum each person expressed their thoughts/feelings regarding the Strengths, Weaknesses, Opportunities, or Threats to the school.

Review before Lunch

Lemniscate Step 3/Eurythmy (Giving and Receiving)
In a large circle, the group "paired off" facing one another. Oranges were distributed, one to each person. To a verse or music, these were "given" with the right hand and "received" with the left hand of the partner.

Lemniscate Step 4/Imagining Alternative Futures
After reflection, participants were to ask themselves: What recent accomplishments were coming from the future: What was yet to be done? What things needed to be changed? What successes from the past could be built upon? Participants were instructed to order their answers in terms of three Dialogues:

> Dialogue with the Spirit
> Dialogue with Each Other
> Dialogue with the Earth (Resources)

Break was not taken. Individuals were asked to get their own coffee, etc., and then return to work.

Lemniscate Step 5/Collaboratively Editing the Vision
Following the presentation in plenum of Alternative Futures by the small groups, those groups were dissolved and participants were free to select one of three affinity groups that formed around each of the dialogue areas:

Dialogue with the Spirit—principles, values, ideals
Dialogue with Each Other—policies, communications
Dialogue with the Earth—site, money, facilities

Groups were to collaboratively edit the vision sheets from the six groups who had just reported into a single grouping without excluding anything.

Closure/Presentation
In plenum, each affinity group presented their edited listings. They appeared to be clear distillations that were harvested from the day's work. Following the presentations there was some time for comment about the process. One sensed that while there was obviously a great deal still to be done, that much had been accomplished during the day.

Comments/Verbatims
Some members expressed amazement that the group went from a "sea" of papers and facts and opinions to a comprehensive, concise vision statement: "How did we wind up with a few, crystal-clear statements from that sea of paper?"

One board member asked for a "reality check": "Are these the vision statements that were really what we want? Is there any disagreement with them?" (Shaking of heads no—no disagreement articulated at that moment.)

Comments from teachers and board members the following week included:

"We published the vision statement in our weekly messenger."

"When I read the vision statements, I still get fired up."

"I think this has done most of the work for the strategic planning process."

8

Development and Fund-raising in Non-Profit Institutions

ROY BUNCE

We must not only give what we have, we must also give what we are.
Desire Mercier

Ask a random sample of people familiar with not-for-profit institutions to list the functions of a development program and the answer will overwhelmingly be, "To raise money." While not false, that is, the task of supporting solicitation lies in the Community Development Program—this answer does point out the degree to which actual community development responsibilities are misunderstood, not only by those who receive solicitation messages, but often by the institutions that benefit from them.

This misunderstanding is supported when we measure the success of the Community Development Program only by dollars raised and ignore the more important community building functions that consume the bulk of development office time and energy and are the very factors that determine whether or not people give. In fact, solicitation is but a part of a whole sphere of interdependent activities that nurture the extended institutional family.

In this chapter we discuss the full range of activities in which a Development Program is engaged. The entire program, including solicitation, should be carefully designed to nurture levels of activity that stimulate individual growth and the maturation of relationships that results in organizational health.

An institution, like a person or family, leads a progressive and cumulative rather than a sequential or linear life. Throughout its life an institution accumulates a history and genealogy until its family network circles the globe and spans the generations. As that network grows, new systems must be put in place to assist and manage its growth.

A look at how institutions fund themselves at different stages of development reveals a general pattern. Chart "A"—"Patterns of School Financial Management"—provides a synopsis of how one institutional type, a school, moves from relying on tuition and occasional fund-raising events to sustain the pedagogical program, to requiring a formal, "donor-centered" Community Development Program to support the broader vision of a more mature institution.

Bear in mind, the Development Program put in place in the administrative phase of an institution's life is the first *formal* program, with staff and funding to support its initiatives, and specific objectives against which to measure its success. However, the fundamentals of a Community Development Program have been present with any institution from the start, perhaps not consciously, and perhaps not always with positive effect, but they have been there.

For example,

- Does the institution maintain facilities that receive the public, its constituents, and/or are visible to the wider community?
- Are student productions open to the public? Does the farm offer public demonstrations? Does the medical center offer public education?
- Do you encourage past "users" of your service to return for special times in the institution's development? Do you help past "users" keep in touch with

each other? Do you maintain contact through a newsletter?

- Do constituent groups participate in associations such as a Parents' Association, an Alumni Association, a Patients' Association?
- Do supporters ever hold an event to raise funds? Do they sponsor a festival or a celebration?
- Does your institution record gifts? Send thank-you notes? Provide donors with IRS documentation?

If you accept the idea that the rationale of a Community Development Program is to stimulate community growth through the strengthening of individuals and relationships, then any and all of the above activities comprise the Community Development Program already in place.

The question then is not, "When do we start a Community Development Program?" but rather, "Where do we stand with the program we already have and what can we do to make it more effective?" "When is it time to pull the piecemeal efforts that tend to react to the current situation into a more unified program that helps in the planning and implementation of programs and activities for the short- and long-term good of the whole?"

The first verbalizing of this question is often made in response to an immediate need for money. Conscious Community Development Programs often manifest when institutions face the need for funding beyond current income as they face a deficit. Or a new building is under construction and there are no funds to pay for it. Then personnel are hired and charged with immediately putting into place a solicitation program.

The problem with turning to solicitation as the first activity to be initiated is that it fails to acknowledge the significance that relationships play in the healthy institution. To rush into solicitation fails to give the donor time to grow in understanding and involvement before being asked to make an investment. It places giving in the forefront of community development activities, rather than as a natural outcome.

When Should We Start a Community Development Program?

The answer to this question lies in the growth patterns common to most institutions—growth in size of the community, growth in program, and growth in physical facilities.

Generally speaking, Community Development Programs derive from:

- *growth in the family of the institution* —when the scale of the family network requires coordinated "management" to support it.
- *the institutional mission*—schools, arts organizations, and health facilities, for example, all promise to provide opportunities for self-investment by all family members.
- *the institution's responsibility to meet certain obligations*— social and legal—toward those who provide support.

Putting a Community Development Program in place shows that the institution recognizes and values its people and takes its responsibility toward them seriously. It also sets the stage for institutional growth and for fund-raising programs and activities.

(CHART A) CHANGING PATTERNS OF
SCHOOL FINANCING AND MANAGEMENT

DEVELOP-MENT STAGE	FUNDING SOURCE	HOUSING NEEDS	FINANCIAL MANAGEMENT	NOTES
Initiative	Founders' invest-ments; Tuition	Minimal, rented facilities; salaries minimal	Part-time staff handles financial management	Program enhancements are provided "benefactors" or by specific, event-centered fund-raising
First Institu-tional Period	Tuition and events; annual fund	More classrooms; larger meeting space; more special teachers	Committees and administrative tasks increasing	Events called on to raise more and more funds for operations, eventually reach-ing their limit.
Second Institu-tional Period	Tuition and events; annual fund; capital investments	Increased specializa-tion of space, faculty, and staff; facility purchased or built	School administrator, development program, and formal board organized	This phase is characterized by consider-able growth in facility to accommodate a more specialized program. Donor-centered solicitation is needed to fulfill institutional goals

Why Have a Community Development Program?

From the management perspective, the scale of the institutional family has changed: there are more people to keep together— an expanding volunteer and family network to support.

The changing economy of scale in a growing institution often calls for more centralized management and more efficient programs. Centralization of the development tasks should leave some staff and volunteers, who have been carrying development functions, free to handle other tasks.

Today, a Community Development Program of the type envisioned is implied in the overall mission of most nonprofit institutions—*to build a healthy community through enabling the self-expression and development of the supporting constituents.* We all define who we are by what we support with our gifts of creativity, energy, and resources, whether the channel of the gift is vocational, personal, family, or communal. An effective Community Development Program does not get people to do something they resist. Rather, it enables individuals to accomplish in concert with others the personal goals they naturally pursue.

The Community Development Program facilitates the process through which the constituency is able to support the institution's focus. The constituent is the Community Development Program's client. The key factors that make possible the constituent's investment are factors of trust, confidence, understanding, and involvement.

The fulfillment of the institution's aims requires that the institution provide:

- a system of governance that is able to reflect the constituents' gifts of *creativity* and reflect to the donor the resultant strengthening of the values they hold;
- a venue within which people may invest their physical *energies* in acts of physical, social, and spiritual significance to their community;

- the opportunity to invest *resources* where they will accomplish the most toward ensuring the fulfillment of institutional goals.

Finally, the Community Development Program fulfills the social and legal responsibilities incumbent upon any person or institution that asks for and receives support. It addresses both protocol and coordination issues. It is through the Community Development Program that volunteers are coordinated to ensure that their actions achieve maximum effect. This coordination ranges from orienting and preparing people to address their task to holding their hand when things do not go as expected.

In the area of protocol, it receives, records, and recognizes all investments of creativity, energy, and resources made in the institution, provides proper legal documentation to the donor, reports on program progress, and seeks to maintain institutional records on the development of community within the institution.

What Does the Community Development Program Do?

The Community Development Program acts as teacher and caregiver to volunteers, historian and guardian of tradition, liaison among its members, and facilitator of transition from generation to generation in both people and programs. It accomplishes these goals as it supports three dialogues: the dialogue with the earth; with resources, buildings, and money; with the soul, with the quality of human relationships and with the spirit; with mission, identity, and values. The energy of Community Development Program staff is directed into serving the institutional family as it participates in those dialogues.

This focus of activity means that the "client" of a Community Development Program is not only the institution but also the alumni, parents, friends, staff, and faculty who seek to make the school, hospital, gallery, a focus of their investment in the world. The Community Development Program insures that constituents have the opportunity to achieve personal meaning through involvement and giving.

The Community Development Program as Teacher

A teacher is a stimulator/coordinator of human experience. A teacher's classroom goal is to stimulate learning and growth in students. To achieve these goals, the teacher must:

- study the student,
- understand the student,
- engage the student,
- inspire the student,
- free the student.

The Community Development Program as teacher follows a similar pattern in fulfilling its mission to provide experiences through which individuals can grow in their relationship to the institution and achieve self-expression through that institution. To that end, the Community Development Program must:

- *Study the constituency it serves*

To effectively encourage a program that supports real institutional needs, the Community Development Program must comprehend the values and goals of the constituency, including the staff, the past and current "users," and the extended family members.

- *Understand the constituency*

Every constituency develops a particular style of operating, its own official tone, politics, and systems and often a behind-the-scene group of individuals who make things happen. It is important that the Community Development Program respond to the relationships among these elements in order to effectively channel information among them and to facilitate the transition of ideas into actions. It must especially understand the decision-making processes of all committees, groups, and boards.

- *Engage the constituency*

Once the Community Development Program understands the constituency, it can facilitate the working together of members of that constituency to benefit the whole. It must be able to guide and support the institutional community as it seeks opportunities for growth through participation (personal investment), and then stand ready to review, select, and receive its family's investments of creativity, energy, and resources. In a well-thought-out plan for the future, the range of opportunities to make such investments is only exceeded by the number of people who would find meaning in sharing your pursuit of a healthier world.

- *Inspire the constituency*

Part of the Community Development Program's role in engaging the constituency lies in helping the community identify leaders in all segments of the community and then supporting their efforts to provide inspiring leadership.

- *Free the individual constituent*

As the constituents, both individually and as a group, grow into and identify more closely with institutional goals, the Community Development Program has a responsibility to help them find avenues for self-expression within the institution. It is the point at which individual constituents share their vision for the future and offer each other the opportunity to invest in the fulfillment of this institutional vision.

The Community Development Program as Caregiver to Volunteers

Volunteers to any cause need to feel that:

1. they are being asked to contribute their energies to an effort that will make a difference;
2. their efforts are critical to success;
3. they will be prepared for and supported in their tasks;
4. their efforts are being coordinated to ensure that the results will equal more than the sum of the parts. They need to know that success can be a reality.

Through festivals and events constituents affirm their relationships and renew their inspiration. Festivals provide opportunities for a community's self-expression, affirmation, and celebration. They make tradition visible in an essential and physical way. We redefine ourselves every time we celebrate as a family. Festivals and events are essential to the community development process and program, though they often do not provide the best vehicle for fund raising. (See the comparison of event- and donor-centered programming—Chart "B.") A great deal of the Community Development Program's time and creativity must center in well-managed festivals and events that serve as catalysts for community growth.

(CHART B) COMPARISON OF EVENT-
AND DONOR-CENTERED FUND-RAISING

EVENT-CENTERED	DONOR-CENTERED
■ Programs focus on an activity such as a telethon, casino night, or recognition dinner. The emphasis is on the activity, not on the needs of the school. There is little learning about the school's needs and goals. ■ Donors quickly forget that they contributed to a cause rather than bought a ticket. There is little association between the event and the sponsor. ■ Events produce little involvement with the school because there is a paucity of information beyond a printed program. The base of support is unchanged and if another event has more appeal next year, the constituency may desert you.	■ A continuous learning process about the school takes place. The more donors know, the more likely they are to share your vision and to give. ■ The constant communication between solicitor and donor helps an informed, educated donor to see that his/her contribution makes a difference. The gift is remembered because the donor gets a positive feeling from giving. ■ After learning about the institution, donors become more involved as their commitment deepens, producing a broad base of continuing support.
■ People buy a ticket for their amusement. ■ There is little carry-over of enthusiasm from the event to the cause because the vital issues are obscured by the event. There is no lasting loyalty or commitment to the cause, even as far as buying a ticket next year.	■ People invest in a better tomorrow. ■ Prospects are insiders with a personal stake in the outcome of a fund-raising program. The emphasis is on developing relations with those whose personal values and sense of community support the goals of the school.

■ There is a built-in ceiling on earnings because of space limitations at the event venue. There is also often a limit on how much you can charge to ensure a profit for the sponsoring organization.	■ The ceiling is as high as the goals you set, and there is no space limitation. How much is given depends on the donor's ability to give, not on the price. There is never a competing event since fund-raising is continuous and convenient to the donor.
■ The donor is asked to give an average amount keyed to the lowest common denominator. While some dinners and other events that focus on a specific rather than general audience offer participation at various levels of giving, there is seldom an effective effort to match the asking with potential.	■ The "asking" is keyed to the institution's need, the donor's ability to give, and the donor's level of commitment/ involvement.
■ "Thons" (ski-a-thons, etc.) have a specific time period after which they are ineffective. The event must be changed if the seasonal deadline is missed.	■ The weather and season do not make any difference. Individual solicitation continues throughout the year.
■ The success of the event is often linked with the personality and personal commitment of one or two individuals in leadership positions at that time. If the leadership changes, the event often must as well.	■ Fund-raising goes on regardless of who happens to be in a specific position of leadership. A change at the top has little effect because the institution, not someone's event, is the focus.
■ Management is riveted to the event itself and the time and place are determined by the event. It is a mass marketing venture with little distinction among individual prospects. It is a "one-shot" gamble for donor dollars.	■ The program management is flexible in terms of time and place because it boils down to one person asking another in a conventional situation. Cultivation, asking and solicitation can be tailored to the knowledge and attitudes of individual prospects. Some will take longer to "buy in" than others.

The Community Development Program
as Historian, Guardian, and Liaison

Any institution is a collection of people, and its biography is the collective biography of all those it serves and those who serve through it. Because of its relationships to the entire body of programs and people, the development office is the natural repository of institutional history, and should be responsible for its collection, maintenance, and dissemination.

Its position at the center of relationships and its role as communicator also make the community development program a guardian of the institution's image—within the institutional community and to the world at large.

Every institution is made up of many people—coworkers, "users," and friends. These individuals become a family, a network of common interest and concerns that invests itself in the cause. This family provides:

- creativity for effective policymaking;
- energy to support the vocational expression;
- resources to fund the physical manifestations of the mission.

The community development program supports the interactions among constituents that join them to the network. Once the community has defined its goals, the community development program works to make visible the vision contained in those goals and helps community members understand the meaning of their support in the achievement of that vision.

The Community Development Program
as Facilitator of Transition

One of the most important functions of the community development program is to help deal with change by facilitating the smooth transfer of volunteer leadership from one generation of volunteers to the next. This facilitation of changes in leadership allows programs to evolve naturally, unencumbered by the fits and starts of changing leadership while making it possible for new people to add new ideas to the program.

The Community Development Program
as Promoter of Planning

Just as it has a responsibility to facilitate transition in people, the community development program also has a duty to facilitate the smooth transition of programs. One means of doing this is to prompt the development and regular updating of a long-range plan. This plan will ensure that the value-centered goals of the whole institution are kept in consciousness in all policy-making decisions.

The Community Development Program
as the Supporter of Solicitation

Solicitation of funds is mainly the responsibility of the constituency: only they, collectively and individually, know what they can and are ready to give. The community development program is responsible for planning, coordinating, and supporting this solicitation process.

Although the development office staff appropriately coordinate the constituency's solicitation, the income received is only one measure of the community development program. Giving is primarily a referendum on:

- the nature and quality of the programs and activities;
- the depth of vision reflected in the institution's long-range plan;
- and, the effectiveness of institutional management and communications.

Giving is a measure of a constituent's connection to the institution and of its commitment to common goals. Gifts also reflect the donor's confidence in the leadership and the management of the institution and its plans for the future. It is important to keep in mind that financial support—whether through annual giving, operating support, endowments, or capital funds—is a measure of the connection, trust, and faith that the constituency has in the institution. In fund-raising activities it is the primary task of the director of development and the community development program to help the board, the development committee, and the carrying group of the institution to seek funds needed for support and to do active solicitation. This relationship suggests that the community development office needs to have the full support of those individuals and groups.

The Community Development Program as a Facilitator of Institutional Dialogue

I have described the many tasks of the community development program and office as facilitating organizational health and renewal so that support—human, spiritual, and financial—can flow toward the institution in order for it to realize its mission. This task means helping the organization to have an active and ongoing dialogue with the spirit, and with the organization's missions and values.

- Is there clarity about mission, values, and goals, and is there a long-range plan that helps the institution translate these into practical steps?
- Have staff, faculty, parents, clients, and friends had an opportunity to participate in the forming and enlivening of the mission and plan?
- Are the mission and plan adequately communicated to the institutional faculty and to the world at large?

The community development office also needs to foster the quality of relationships, of the soul life of the initiative.

- Are internal relationships healthy?
- Do committees and decision-making groups work well and with clarity and purpose?
- Are parents, clients, or customers welcomed into the organization?
- Is the organization exclusive or inclusive in gesture?
- Are there adequate celebrations of institutional and festival life?
- Is there an opportunity for people to get to know each other?
- Are conflicts worked with effectively?
- Are donors, volunteers, and supporters seen and honored?
- Is the memory of individual gifts of creativity and finances retained in a conscious manner?
- Is the life of the institution and its achievements honored?

Last is the dialogue with the earth, with buildings, tasks, budgets, salaries, fees, donations, organizational systems and procedures. Through this dialogue constituents awaken to:

- What human and spiritual values are reflected in budgets.
- What statements budgets make about institutional intent.
- What we consciously tell the world about ourselves in the information we distribute about ourselves.
- What we unconsciously tell the world about ourselves in the way we answer the phone, greet visitors, and in the signs we hang that enable visitors to move within our space.
- How people know whom to call for what.

- How people know where they "need to be on Friday morning."
- How people are kept informed of developments within the institution that affect them and the future of the cause.
- How institutional decisions are made. By whom. How decision-makers come into their positions. How the decision-making process can be made visible.

A formal, conscious community development program, as we have seen, initiates and supports the activities that stimulate growth in the individuals and groups that make up the institutional family. The forces released through individual growth are forces through which institutions grow and become healthy. A community development program is an important vehicle for bringing healing into our institutions and helps the institution to attract the support needed to realize its aims.

In the third chart (Chart "C"), the practical activities of the community development office are described using a school as the example, although similar development activities are essential for all non-profit organizations. It does not describe the further range of activities needed for planning and running a capital campaign that represents a qualitatively much larger effort for the development office and the institution. If the development activity can help these dialogues remain healthy and in development, if it can foster these dialogues with the spirit, with people, and with the earth, then the human and financial resources needed for future activity will be available.[1]

---

1. See *Give to Live, How Giving Can Change Your Life*, by Douglas M. Lawson, Ph.D. (ALTI Publishing, 1991), for many inspiring examples of the gifting process. Also Harold Seymour, *Designs for Fundraising* (McGraw Hill, 1978). Thomas Broce's book, *Fundraising: A Guide to Raising Money from Private Sources* (University of Oklahoma Press, 1988), has more of a technical how-to focus. Also see Michael Phillips, *The Seven Laws of Money*, (NY: Random House, 1974).

(CHART C) Development Office Responsibility at Four Levels of Institutional Life

PROGRAMS	PHYSICAL LEVEL	SYSTEMIC LEVEL	RELATIONAL LEVEL		WILL
Parent Relations	•Record relational activities	•Work toward smooth transition of leadership •Maintain ongoing review of management systems of institution to insure they meet constituents' needs •Plan, coordinate, and evaluate events and provide catalyst to develop sense of family	•Run events such as open houses/class parties •Provide catalyst to development of sense of family		•Provide conduit of information regarding investment opportunities
Alumni Relations	•Record relational activities	•Work toward smooth transition of leadership •maintain ongoing review of management systems of institution to ensure they meet constituents' needs •Plan, coordinate and evaluate events and provide catalyst to develop sense of family	•Run events •Provide catalyst to development of sense of family	•Ensure accurate focus and presentation of institutional will	•Provide conduit of information regarding investment opportunities
Volunteer Enlistment	•Track enlistment process •Provide background on prospects to enlisters	•Prepare job descriptions •Evaluate volunteer performance	•Support enlistment of key volunteers	•Provide "bio-feedback" to the constituency on the success and opportunities and to ensure that individuals have the opportunity to invest their wills and to keep individuals in the "meaning loop"	•Individuals make personal and free gifts of their energy and creativity
Publications	•Ensure ready supply of long-shelf life publications: Annual Report, Viewbooks, Catalogues	•Prepare rosters •Develop recognizable image/logo and typeface	•Produce Annual Report to reflect contributions of creativity, energy, and resources by members of the constituency		•Produce Annual Report to reflect accomplishments of the institutional will
Public Relations	•Scout institution for PR opportunities: read bulletinboards/newspapers, listen •Read constituent public newspapers for extra-institution activities of family •Prepare news releases to public media	•Acquaint people with daily life of the institution	•Create articles that help people understand the institution's broadest goals and visions		•Focus public relations to illustrate the institutional will/mission
Communications	•Prepare/distribute, in a timely fashion, newsletters/weekly bulletins, etc. •Ensure readability of all printed materials	•Develop recognizable image/ logo and typeface	•Recognize leadership •Ensure the distribution of information to support constituents in the fulfillment of their relationship tasks		•Focus communications according to the institutional will/mission
Solicitation Annual Fund Capital	•Track solicitation process •Provide background on prospects to solicitors •Prepare regular reports to keep workers informed of progress	•Train volunteers in solicitation procedures •Ensure effective interface with business office	•Prepare volunteers to address solicitation issues/to enter solicitation event •Volunteers speak with peers leading them to a new level of ownership of the institution's goals		•Individuals make personal and free gifts of themselves through financial resources •Thank all donors
General Administration	•Computer: file management/ maintenance •Office supplies: Maintenance •Maintain up-to-date mailing lists •Handle incoming phone calls/mail				

III

Signs of Hope

Imaginations for a Better Future

9

Initiatives and
Individual Development

CHRISTOPHER SCHAEFER

All men are caught in an inescapable network of mutuality,
tied in a single garment of destiny. Whatever affects one
directly affects all indirectly. I can never be what I ought to be
until you are what you ought to be, and you can never be
what you ought to be until I am what I ought to be.

Martin Luther King

Soul Development through Initiatives:
the Dialogue with the Earth

A way of approaching the question of individual development
in initiatives is to go back to the beginning of our exploration
and to recall the three dialogues that we regarded as central to
both individual and organizational health. One was the dialogue with the earth, with matter, finances, buildings. The second was the dialogue with people, while the third was the
dialogue with the spirit. If, as initiative-takers, we take the dialogue with the earth as relating to the struggle to found, build,
maintain, and develop organizations, then we can readily see
how we are continuously challenged to develop and deepen
our capacities.

The process of initiative-taking has already been described
in some detail. If one looks at what is entailed in such a process, then one can say that initiative-takers require the ability
to perceive what is needed and respond with confidence and

flexibility to this need. In addition they need to possess both courage and persistence.

Is the perceived need real or an individual pipe dream? Only the response of the public will tell. I remember sitting in an office in late spring mailing the brochures of a new social training course to many parts of the world and having the sinking feeling that perhaps no one would want to come. Only when applications began arriving and we had eighteen participants for our first course did we know that there was a real interest.

Even if the need is real, the ability to respond to it requires great inner flexibility, not to speak of long hours and sacrifice. Temporary buildings, a different location, part-time outside work, or a modification of product or service may be required. A compromise with reality, with the earth, is asked for and this sorely tests our resolve. A training center for young people, which was intended for a rural setting, ended up on the main street of a small English town; and a Waldorf school that wished for spacious pleasant surroundings had to rent antiquated premises in Chicago. These steps required compromise, a modification of expectations, but they made life possible.

The qualities of courage and persistence are equally vital. The initiative begins with nothing except an idea and perhaps some friends. In taking an initiative, we are going into the unknown with only ourselves as resources. Subconsciously and sometimes consciously we feel that we may fail and be exposed to ridicule or criticism. So a threshold of fear needs to be crossed, not only once but repeatedly. In other cases the fear of success may play in. If we succeed, then we have to take ourselves more seriously and perhaps become responsible for larger tasks. I believe that fear is the cause of many aborted initiatives and of many which die in infancy. However, if we dare to start, and to continue, then we acquire, use, and build courage.

In addition to courage, the "long will" is needed—the quality of perseverance and patience. Fortunately, we are not able to see all the obstacles that the initiative will encounter in its life before we start, otherwise we probably would never begin.

I believe the points mentioned are obvious for anyone who has ever been involved in starting something. As is frequently pointed out, initiatives "build character." By stepping back and reflecting on our experiences we can see that initiatives are a training ground for our faculties of soul.

If clear perception, courage, flexibility, and the long will are the inner qualities called for in the early years of the initiative, then clarity, delegation of responsibility, and attention to detail are vital in the administrative phase. Many individuals do not have the inclination to move from the earlier, heroic period to the more functional, orderly administrative phase. An inner redirection is required that can be very painful for pioneering individuals in particular, as it means giving up the role of the parent, the provider. Yet if such a transition can be made, there is much to be gained from the more rational, clear, orderly, and defined world of tasks and relationships called for in this new phase of development.

The integrated organization calls for additional inner qualities—a new process consciousness, which entails working in a collaborative, associative manner with subcontractors, suppliers, and clients and being able to exercise an ennobling developmental leadership in which furthering and assisting others becomes central. Becoming process- and other-directed rather than task- and self-directed is a stretch for anyone and reflects qualities of true wisdom.

We can see that the development of organizations calls upon the best qualities that each phase of human development has to offer us:

1. The courage, initiative, will, and enthusiasm of youth: the *Pioneer Phase.*

2. The clarity, rationality, planning, and attention to life of adulthood and middle age: the *Administrative Phase.*

3. The wisdom, life consciousness, insight, and compassion of maturity: the *Integrated Mature Organization.*[1]

By indicating this natural relationship between the phases of life and the development phases of organizations, I am not saying that only the young pioneer can create new ventures or the old create an integrated organization. Many people in their fifties begin new careers or organizations. I know of several individuals who began very successful pioneer ventures in their sixties. The opposite is also true; younger people with incredible social gifts take an organization in the crisis of the administrative phase into the culture of a new process organization. However, this natural relationship between the phases of individual and of organization development does exist. If we have had the good fortune of working in organizations in different stages of development, then we know how each stage calls upon different inner qualities.

Working with Others as an Aspect of Inner Development =
The Dialogue with People

Many newly created institutions embody the ideals of working together for worthwhile aims. A measure of equality is often sought and aspects of mutual interdependence are acknowledged. And yet it often appears to be so hard to work together, to achieve agreement, and to create a positive collegial environment. One of the reasons for this difficulty is that we all naturally possess strong self-centered anti-social qualities.

---

1. See Paul Eugen Schiller, *Rudolf Steiner and Initiation* (Anthroposophic Press, 1981). Refer to chapter 1 of this book.

If we focus on the mirroring, balancing function that working relationships provide for us, then one of the most obvious benefits is bringing these self-interested, antisocial qualities to awareness. If we pay careful attention to our thought life when listening to another person, we can notice that we selectively listen to what we agree or disagree with and then busily formulate a response. Observing our thoughts more closely, we can see the quality of doubt, of critical intelligence directed at the thoughts of others.

If we observe our feelings, we can notice that our relationships are colored by a sea of likes and dislikes. There are some people in a working group whom I naturally like, agree with, and enjoy, and others with whom I have difficulty, no matter what they do. These likes and dislikes are not only the basis for judgments about others, but often also the basis of far-reaching decisions. Yet such feelings are usually quite unreliable, as they tend to say more about what we like or don't like about ourselves than anything objective about the other. These natural likes and dislikes can be the greatest enemies of true social life since they often block the development of real interest between people, hindering the search for a deeper, conscious understanding of human relationships. The picture that has sometimes come to my mind regarding these forces of sympathy and antipathy is that they give rise to a butterfly collector mentality in us—they tempt us to categorize and then pin people to particular images. Once done, it is impossible for anyone to escape—"Tom is always late, isn't he?"—and we needn't actually concern ourselves with individuals any more. They are, after all, already categorized in our private collection.[2]

---

2. For a penetrating description of these difficulties see Rudolf Steiner, "How Can the Psychological Distress of Today Be Overcome?" in *Spiritual Research: Methods and Results* (Blauvelt, NY: SteinerBooks, 1981).

If we observe our behavior, our intentions, something of our will in a group, we can quickly notice that when we get our way we are pleased, gracious, even open, but when we do not, we react in a variety of negative ways. At this more subtle and less conscious level of the soul a certain selfishness and egotism reigns, even when couched in terms of wanting what is good for others or for the community. Marjorie Spock discusses this issue at some length in her wonderful essay, *Reflections on Community Building.*[3]

Through working with others we can come to recognize these fundamental antisocial forces in our soul:

- Doubt and criticism in our thought life,
- Sympathy and antipathy in our feeling life,
- Egotism and selfishness in our will life.

While these soul forces lead us to greater self-consciousness, they can also block a genuine meeting with others.

Knowing about our antisocial nature is, of course, not adequate—it must be repeatedly experienced and ultimately *accepted* if we are even to consider a future transformation. For this transformation to happen it is not only important that individuals review their daily experiences, but that groups and institutions review their meetings and the quality of their working relationships. Only through a process of reviewing meetings and decisions can we begin to remind each other what we have achieved and not achieved, recall our antisocial nature, and gradually build that loyalty and caring that makes mutual development possible.

A second balancing factor to be experienced in our new living and working arrangements is a growing individual

---

3. Marjorie Spock, *Reflections on Community Building.* Self-published. This excellent essay contains many important insights on human relationships. Available through Anthroposophic Press, Hudson, NY.

awareness of our untransformed sides. Jung refers to this part of the soul as the "shadow" and Rudolf Steiner calls it the "double." Especially in conflict situations we can notice that suddenly we are consumed by anger or hatred. In some people this appears primarily as heat, as a violent mood that arises within, overwhelming all common sense. In others, there may be a cold, manipulative hatred that seeks to inflict pain. Often both qualities are present. In this experience we see something of the faces of evil. To acknowledge the presence of such qualities as "mine," as requiring transformation and inner development, is to begin to take spiritual beings—including ourselves—seriously.

So far, we have concentrated on how human relationships and working groups can provide balance through making us aware of our antisocial nature, and of our untransformed "double." This reflecting mirror function is an essential service we can perform for each other, no matter how badly or semiconsciously, and it is an activity for which we can also feel gratitude.

The mirror function of working groups and of conscious relationships can be seen as a call to see ourselves more clearly and to develop. Fortunately, another quality is also present when we live and work with each other over time—an invitation to develop interest, understanding, and, ultimately, the beginnings of love. This invitation is subtle and only becomes apparent over time. We may notice that a particular person always brings the discussion back to a point that we left ten minutes ago. At first this retreat is annoying, perhaps even maddening, but then one day we notice the important clarifications that result. We become interested, we listen to how the person expresses his or her thoughts, how this annoying quality can work positively, as well as negatively. This spark of initial interest is a door through which we can proceed. We may ask what temperament, what background, what life history expresses itself in this person? In short, we seek some understanding of the other.

The more we learn the more we appreciate how different people are, how fundamentally other is their experience of the world. This process can lead to a friendship and the thought, "How wonderful that they are different—that there are differences between people." Perhaps some weeks or months later, when we are facing an important decision in the group, the same person again brings up an issue left behind long ago, this time in such a way that others react badly. The resulting injury to that person leads us to act. After the meeting we go to the person, we discuss the incident and share some of our observations, not out of anger but out of understanding and compassion.

We all have experiences of this kind but perhaps don't realize their importance. Initially, when we begin to listen, we are turning our thought consciousness outward—turning doubt into interest—moving from a closed gesture to an open one. This turning of thought into active listening—into interest— requires effort. It is a willing-thinking listening process. Once accomplished, it often activates our feeling toward the other, transforming our natural sympathies and antipathies into an organ of perception, into a feeling of empathy and of objective sympathy. This transformation of thought and feelings is important in social life, for the butterfly collection in our soul is a kind of coffin for others, making them unfree. To rid ourselves of fixed images of others, to develop a picture based on warm understanding, carrying in it a recognition of the other's striving spirit—and of that which they are struggling to transform—is a vital social deed.

A warm and empathetic understanding of another person in our feeling life can then also fire the will, transforming egoistic impulses into deeds of compassion and, ultimately, of love.

The "mirror" and "invitation" functions of working with others in connection with individual development can be summarized in the following manner:

THE MIRROR		THE INVITATION
Doubt	*thinking*	Interest Attention
Sympathies and Antipathies	*feeling*	Empathetic Understanding
Egotism	*willing*	Deeds of Compassion

AWARENESS OF ANTISOCIAL FORCES

DEVELOPMENT OF SOCIAL FORCES

The Double   The Ego

As experiences, the mirror and the invitation are not sequential. Sometimes genuine interest in another can make us aware that we have in the past not listened but have met his or her thoughts with doubt. Sometimes it is the other way around; the awareness of our antisocial side creates a mood of humility that leads to genuine interest.[4]

In looking at this process of relating to others, it is important to recognize a basic polarity. In meeting others we are, as it were, oscillating between being awake in ourselves, formulating responses, attending to our feelings—the antisocial forces— and attending to others, listening to them and living into their reality—the social forces. This swing between waking to ourselves and attending to others is natural and can be observed in every conversation we have. To develop new social forces our consciousness must be strong enough to maintain awareness

---

4. Christopher Schaefer, "The Highest Art," in *Breakthrough*, the Journal of the Global Education Association.

while listening to and understanding others. As in all inner development, this listening activity requires a continuous and conscious struggle. A small indication of this struggle is the experience of how tiring it is to truly listen to another person for a period of time—and how enlivening to listen to oneself. I think that the practice of maintaining consciousness while using one's soul faculties of thinking, feeling, and willing to understand the other is analogous to maintaining consciousness in sense-free meditation. Such deep understanding is indeed a social meditation, a new sacrament.

The task of developing conscious social qualities is important for the individual, for others, and for initiatives. Who has not had at least one experience of being truly listened to and felt the warmth, enjoyed the resulting clarity of thought, and experienced the wonder of a true conversation? At still another level, to live and work with others who carry a true picture of ourself is to be continuously encouraged in the struggles of life. Perhaps most important, groups of people who are striving to develop conscious social qualities have the possibility of helping to fulfill each other's destiny. The antisocial qualities block a recognition of true human possibilities. More conscious social qualities and relationships create an open space in which individual strengths, weaknesses, and potentials can be mutually worked out.

For groups and initiatives seeking to serve the needs of the time, the individual development of new social faculties is the leaven that makes such service possible. The essential relationship between the phases of an organization's development and the type of consciousness required in the pioneer, differentiation, and integration phases has already been discussed. The more fundamental connection between the aims and morality of the initiative and the aims, morality, and social awareness of the initiative-takers is evident upon reflection. We cannot serve positive aims or goals in freedom without a substantial measure of self-awareness and social understanding.

Development in Life and the Dialogue with the Spirit

I have tried to suggest that consciously taking initiatives implies a process of individual development. The aspects of such development include exercising new soul faculties, achieving moments of inner quiet, recognizing our antisocial nature, and developing a new understanding of others. These opportunities for greater self-awareness and self-transformation are given to us every day. Yet it is not automatic, for we need to consciously recognize that we are on the road with others and be willing to work with and share the challenges along the way. Individual development in and through life is different from, though connected to, a conscious inner path of spiritual work. Development in life focuses on understanding our life experiences and gradually transforming ourselves as a result in order to become better, more conscious human beings.[5]

An inner path of meditative development involves an effort to practice a conscious relationship to the spirit. For some this may mean working out of a religious tradition and engaging in daily prayer, asking for the strength and insight to be a vessel of the spirit. For others it may entail regularly focussing on a meditative content in order to gradually unfold the capacity of spiritual cognition. In either case, there is the need to acknowledge a higher spiritual world and to know this recognition through reflection, prayer, and meditation. If we wish ourselves and our organizations to be a "gift to the spirit," as Max Depree calls it, then we must also find some way of engaging in this activity with our colleagues—perhaps by working with a favorite verse, sharing a profound thought or meditation, or engaging in the joint study of spiritual content.[6]

---

5. See Bernard Lievegoed, *Towards the 21st Century, Doing the Good* (Toronto: Rudolf Steiner Publications, 1983).
6. Max Depree, *Leadership is an Art* (Doubleday, 1990), pp. 61–62.

I personally think that just as our body and soul are the vessel for our higher self, so too is an organization a vessel for a spirit. If this thought is true, then how can we nurture this being and establish a relationship with it? What I experience is that an attitude of wanting to serve and of listening is critical. What is wanted of us in this school, therapy center, farm cooperative, or small business by the spirit of our venture? I believe we can and must ask for guidance and offer our thoughts, intentions, and deeds as nourishment to the higher world. Such a listening and offering is true of my relationship with my higher self and it is also true for our relationship to the spirit being of our organization. How we practice this dialogue with the spirit individually and collectively will depend on our spiritual orientation, but that we must practice this conversation is vital if we are to be responsible co-creators of the natural and social world. The moral qualities of our individual and organizational life are the ground from which such a dialogue with the spirit proceeds.

Moments of Reflection

In looking at the conscious development of initiatives, the importance of stepping back from the pressures of the everyday and reviewing what has happened in the past and what is wanted for the future was repeatedly stressed. This periodic extended review and planning time involves developing an objective picture of the initiative's biography, its past strengths and weaknesses, and formulating a joint and consciously-willed picture of the future. Behind such a suggestion is the idea that we learn most by consciously reviewing and digesting our experiences and then projecting forward the lessons learned.

While engaging in such periodic reflections about the initiative, we can become much more aware of our role in it and how our personality affects it. While reviewing the functioning of an institution I was involved with in England, I noticed that one of its areas of weakness was that it paid little attention to administrative practices and that it had limited rhythm and regularity in its staff and administrative meetings. On further reflection, I became aware of my own desk, my dislike of paperwork, and my interest in new meetings and projects. The connection seemed to be more than coincidental, and I was forced to work with it. Indeed, I have found the connection between the character of an initiative and the strengths and weaknesses of the founding personalities to be so striking that often just creating an awareness of it will lead to substantial individual and institutional change.

Such moments of reflection in the life of the initiative can clearly bring greater self-knowledge as well as being essential to the healthy development of the venture. We can consciously extend this principle to the rest of our lives by choosing to create periods of quiet reflection. In so doing, we are meeting one of the conditions of inner development—creating moments of inner tranquillity—in which we have the possibility of distinguishing the essential from the nonessential in our lives. Through such a practice in our initiatives and in our lives we gain greater understanding and increase our strength to serve moral human goals.

PRACTICAL EXERCISES FOR SELF-DEVELOPMENT

from the Work of Rudolf Steiner

The six exercises are as follows and are to be practiced sequentially, adding later ones when familiarity has been achieved with earlier ones.

1. The Mastery of Thought Life:

The individual is asked to determine the sequence of his or her thoughts by focusing attention on simple objects, such as the origin, function, and make-up of a paper clip, a pencil, or a candle. By practicing for an extended period of time, i.e., 5 to 10 minutes daily, the tendency to wander in one's thoughts and to have unrealistic conceptions can be overcome so that thoughts will more reflect inner effort and have a relation to the object being contemplated.

2. The Mastery over Will Impulses:

Rarely do will impulses originate in conscious intentions. Rudolf Steiner therefore suggests giving oneself a small but conscious task at a given point during the day—for example, retying a shoelace at 4 p.m. What matters is the perseverance and the exactitude with which we accomplish such tasks, adding more and more consciousness to our will life daily.

3. Equanimity in Our Feeling Life:

This exercise can be repeatedly practiced and is directed at not letting feeling dominate one's life and reactions. Moments of joy and sorrow are part of life, but often they overtake us, leading to excessive actions or moods. The point is to maintain inner composure within the vicissitudes of life through practicing equanimity and balance in our feelings.

4. Positivity in Judgments about People and the World:

We are often confronted with life situations where judgments are made about the quality of work done, tardiness at meetings, or an argument between colleagues. This exercise suggests reviewing such situations and seeing people and life in a broader context. A person may be habitually late, but a closer look reveals that he is always responding to other people's needs. An accident is not only hurtful but may lead to something important and new in life. We have the opportunity of practicing a conscious positivity and understanding many times a day, thereby avoiding getting into fixed and often negative positions and judgments.

5. Lack of Preconceptions or Openness in Understanding Life:

Here it is suggested that we practice being open to that which is new; a different opinion, a new person, an unusual request, or a new way of developing one's initiative.

6. The Harmonious Balance between These Attributes:

The six exercises should not be developed in a one-sided way, and it is for that reason that it is suggested doing just one every day for a month and then moving on to a second, a third, and so on; or adding a second one the second month until all six are being worked with.

The exercises may appear simple. By doing them it will be observed that far from being easy, they demand repeated effort. It is best to try them and see what effects they have on your outer and inner life. Such an effort will, I believe, reveal their central relevance in taking initiatives; they reinforce the learning we are continuously confronted with in our working lives.

Adapted from Rudolf Steiner's
Occult Science, An Outline

10

Signs of Hope

Imaginations for the Future

TŸNO VOORS AND

CHRISTOPHER SCHAEFER

> No problem where to begin. Wherever you are is the
> entry point.
>
> *Harry Wilmer*

Brian Thorne, in an address to the British Association for
Counselling, gave expression to a deep concern as well as a
hope for the future of humanity, which we share.

> I believe that we need to have faith that, despite so many
> indications to the contrary, we are living in an age when we
> are poised on the threshold of a momentous phase in our
> evolution, our evolution as a species. Either we shall take
> a great leap forward or we shall fall into a ditch of such
> depth that the days of Noah will be repeated on the face
> of the earth.[1]

The signs of psychological, social, and economic distress are
obvious in a heartbreaking fashion, from violence and starva-
tion in Bosnia and the civil wars in Africa to the unemployment
and homelessness in many Western societies. Yet there are also
many signs of hope, of courageous and inspired efforts to

---

1. Brian Thorne, *Person-Centered Counselling* (Whurr Publisher, 1991), p. 158.

respond to human need and to reform our social, economic, and educational systems by building organizations and communities based on new human and spiritual values. The list of encouraging initiatives is legion: the work of Co-op America, of Amnesty International; of micro-banking in the developing world, the growth of peer assistance networks in North American schools, the spread of ethical investment and a new ecological consciousness; the growth of Waldorf education, of new forms of work and business practice through The Other Economic Summit (TOES), the World Business Academy, the Schumacher Society, and the Social Venture Network. In the following pages a number of initiatives are described in more detail. They have been chosen because they are positive examples of social transformation. It is our hope that they can enliven the imagination to creatively work on the many challenges that we face in our time.

ARTA: A Therapeutic Community for Drug Rehabilitation (Holland)

One of the distressing symptoms of our time is the fact that so many people are out of work for a long time, or homeless, while others have become totally dependent on drugs or alcohol. As a result, many have lost all sense of identity, all sense for life. We can also observe that increasingly people are engaged in a variety of ways to meet and help these problems. Successful initiatives in this realm often form communities that initially serve as a refuge. These life or work communities gradually become a home in which people can reconnect with themselves and develop confidence to meet and engage with the world.

One such initiative is the life and work community, ARTA, in Zeist, Holland. When ARTA started in 1976, a group of people had already been working for a long time to develop a therapeutic program for former drug addicts. From 1981 they developed their present program that leads former addicts through a process of four phases, which are a kind of repetition of the phases of childhood.[2]

In so doing, the disturbances in the normal development of childhood can be corrected by people themselves, thereby opening the way to finding new life aims and directions.

The first phase starts on a farm. Old habits and life-styles are exchanged for a rhythmic structure of the day. Everyone—co-workers and participants—engages in the daily farm life, the care of the animals, the garden and the house, and the preparation of the meals.

The second phase starts when people can live without the drugs, and a new life rhythm is found. In this phase new life-forces must be built up. Central to this is rhythm and work. Morning and late afternoon are for work in the garden, wood workshop, weavery, or house and kitchen. In the afternoon, participants are engaged in different medical therapies to build up their vitality. Evenings are filled with biographical conversations, and the telling of myths and legends.

The third phase is an intensification of this program, aimed toward the discovery of one's own strengths and weaknesses. In work, participants are asked to take more responsibility—meals must be served on time, tools must be clean, workshops ready for the next day. The afternoons are filled with different artistic therapies, such as painting, drawing, modeling, massage. Participants are also invited to start studying to awaken their interest and to challenge their thinking and individual judgment. The evenings are spent on topical social questions, drama, and prepared talks and evaluation.

In the fourth phase, work-and-study-programs are gradually exchanged for placement periods in companies or other institutions, or in vocational training programs. Participants are freer to arrange their time but at the same time become responsible for an area of work. Weekends are spent on nature

2. Bernard Lievegoed, *Phases* (London: Rudolf Steiner Press, 1993).

walks, visiting museums, or going to the theater. Participants in the fourth phase are responsible for such weekend programs.

Gradually the participant finds his or her direction as well as the confidence to leave ARTA. A departure can take place when a healthy place to live has been found, and a meaningful work or training established.

Around this program, carried by the therapeutic community, the coworkers have developed a social and spiritual community to enable them to gain support for each other and to nurture the impulse they want to serve. The social community organizes itself through the mandate- principle described in chapter 5.

ARTA can be seen as an initiative that works out of a deep care and respect for the individual human being.

Similar initiatives have started in Germany, Sweden, and the U.S.A.

Gifts of Love, Inc.:
A Volunteer Group of Families Helping Families[3] (U.S.A.)

Gifts of Love is a private nonprofit social service agency. It started two and one-half years ago, and has expanded from one family helping another to include an emergency food pantry, and a community service organization helping over 800 families each month. We would like to give some examples of what, with your help, Gifts of Love has been able to accomplish.

Gifts of Love was able to collect and deliver more than 600 stuffed animals to an inner city elementary school with less than eleven days notice! It is an organization that collected 260 personal care kits with all kinds of "extras" in them plus hundreds of other items to be assembled into kits in the future. These kits were delivered to shelters and agencies that help to

---

3. From *The Sunroom*, The Gifts of Love Newsletter, vol. 1, Summer, 1991.

feed the hungry and the lines to receive them were quite long. As happy as we were to be passing them out, we were saddened by the number of people we were unable to help, at this time. We have decided to schedule this project more than once a year, due to the many beautiful letters from agency directors thanking us and expressing their hopes for future supplies of these items.

Gifts of Love also provides emergency food to families in the cities referred through their social service workers. Some of these people have arrived from Puerto Rico and are awaiting city assistance for a week or two. Or perhaps they were the victims of a crime or fire and have to wait days to receive insurance money or state assistance. We are able to help with donated food, or using your donated dollars, to send a volunteer to feed these less fortunate people, give them diapers and soap, and even perhaps clothes and toys. We have donated furniture, televisions, dishes, towels, and even a kitchen sink! All of these items are provided at no charge and are delivered by our very kindhearted volunteers. We also match families during holidays so you can choose to directly sponsor a less fortunate family and deliver your holiday meal and gifts, and, if you desire, visit with them.

Gifts of Love, however, reaches into your world, too. We do not service just the inner cities. With the economy in its current state of bleakness (especially in New England) we are helping many more of your friends, neighbors and old coworkers than anyone could ever imagine! We receive calls daily from people who have depleted their savings, their pantries, and their relatives' savings trying to save their homes. It is very difficult for them to call because they were often the people who always donated. They cry, they hug, they are bitter but they need help. Sometimes they refuse help from their church or synagogue because they do not want to be known as "the people who need help." So they suffer. Some eat only water and ketchup or hunt in their yards until the pains of hunger become unbearable. Then they call Gifts of Love. Since we are a private program we can use our discretion and help them even if they have their own home and are trying to save it. Sometimes they are going through a foreclosure, and are hoping and praying that a job or a house sale will relieve them of the misery they are experiencing. Yes, they live in Simsbury, Avon, Farmington, all suburbs of Hartford, Connecticut.

The Door: A Center for Alternatives,
Comprehensive Services for Inner City Youth[4] (U.S.A.)

The Door was founded in 1972 as a project of the International Center for Integrative Studies (ICIS). The concept behind The Door grew out of recommendations of a task force of young professionals who wanted to give practical application to the integrative philosophy of its organization. Members of the task force, from their varying perspectives on health, mental health, education, law, and the arts, felt a new approach was needed to meet the needs of inner-city teenagers. Existing social service agencies were financially, geographically, or psychologically inaccessible, or provided only fragmented, single-service care (The Door Report, 1987).

Thus, The Door was founded in large measure to help New York City's teenagers cut through bureaucratic obstacles in order to get the help they needed. From the beginning, The Door took a stance of providing services in a comprehensive and integrative way so young people could benefit from the knowledge of professionals from many different disciplines all located within a single facility. When young people visit The Door they are assigned a primary counselor to monitor their involvement. Then they are encouraged to explore any program available that might help them to solve their problems or enrich their experience. They might work directly with a variety

---

4. Suzanne Schecker, from *New Synthesis Think Tank Papers*, 1987.

of people: doctors, lawyers, nurses, social workers, teachers, job developers, counselors, master artists, athletic coaches and more.

Services and programs are coordinated through nightly team meetings where, in a collective effort, professional staff share their perspectives on the needs and problems of individual Door members. These team meetings are the key to the workings of The Door's integrated services philosophy. In the course of these meetings, as a doctor consults with an art teacher, a social worker with a nutritionist, or perhaps, a lawyer with an athletic coach, staff come to a fuller, more holistic understanding of each person's needs (The Door Report, 1987).

Dealing with the whole person, acknowledging physical, emotional, intellectual, interpersonal, and spiritual dynamics makes it possible to go beyond the youth's obvious problems and to explore special growth dimensions as well. The following services are available to aid in this growth:

- a comprehensive health program staffed by physicians, nurses and other medical staff.
- family planning and sex counseling services.
- a prenatal, young parents, and child program.
- nutrition counseling, food services, and a cafeteria.
- social services, crisis intervention, and runaway counseling.
- a mental health counseling and therapy program.
- an education program with counseling, tutoring, remediation, language training, and treatment of learning disabilities.
- career counseling, vocational training and job placement.
- legal advice, counseling, and advocacy.
- arts, crafts, music, theater and dance programs and workshops.
- recreation and martial arts programs and facilities.

The Door's Creative and Physical Arts Program is made up of the Visual Arts, the Physical Arts, and the Performing Arts. These programs are staffed and supervised by practicing professionals and are so popular that the staff cannot keep up with the demand. Members have the opportunity to develop their talents from the beginning to professional levels, and realistic career goals and employment opportunities are emphasized. In addition to marketing their abilities as artists, performers, or athletes, young people explore related fields such as lighting, sound engineering, publicity, arts management, teaching, and coaching.

A cafeteria is operated at The Door, which provides training for young people in all aspects of running it as a business: buying the food, cooking, waitressing, and cashiering. In fact, in managing The Door, as many operations as possible are performed by the program members, including servicing the front desk.

To thousands of adolescents The Door has become a place where they can come with confidence in a crisis or for continuing care. They come from throughout New York's five boroughs as well as from the suburbs, adjacent states, and even at times from other countries. Some have heard about The Door from friends, others are referred by schools, hospitals, community agencies, courts, and drug treatment programs. The clients are drawn from all ethnic backgrounds and they range in age from 12 to 20, with the majority between the ages of 15 and 18.

Adolescence is a time of extremely rapid change when young people are struggling to establish their personal and sexual identity, a sense of self-esteem and competence, satisfactory interpersonal relationships, and increasing independence. Many of the people who come to The Door have emotional, family, medical, job, or school related problems. Some are drug or alcohol abusers and others face crises such as pregnancy, trouble with the law, or running away from home. Generally, they have heard that The Door is a good place with services they can use.

Since its inception, The Door has emphasized the value of a holistic and human approach, within the context of an intensive working relationship between young people and staff. Within a decade, it has moved to the forefront among the nation's youth service agencies. It is being replicated in New York City and State, Washington D.C., Mexico, Guatemala, Canada, Bermuda, the Virgin Islands, the Philippines, and Australia, with an ever growing list of countries around the world.

In the past fifteen years more than 100,000 teenagers have visited The Door, each bringing, and in turn discovering, something special. The Door fosters activities that are stimulating, require discipline and commitment, and provide youth with a sense of community. Young people who participate can look forward to the satisfaction that comes with a sense of achievement, dignity, and belonging. The Door offers them meaningful opportunities to express themselves, to develop new interest, and to find self-worth. (The Door Report, 1987).

> At The Door we find that despite their problems, which can be many and deep-seated, disadvantaged inner-city young people are often highly intelligent and wise in practical knowledge. They possess vitality, idealism, team spirit, and untapped creative potential. Their image in this country is that of being a threat to society, as if they are the cause of society's problems rather than its victims. We feel that the image should be reversed: young people are a rich resource. They are, after all, our hope for the future (The Door Report, 1986).

Forum 3: A Youth and Life Center (Germany)

Forum 3 in Stuttgart, Germany, is a unique place of vitality and openness. Forum 3 started in 1969 at the time of the Prague Spring. A small group of architects, actors, and craftspeople realized there was a need for a meeting place, a forum. The place became known and gathered many young people who felt there was a sympathetic ear for their ideas and problems. Activities developed and at present the "tearooms" are a central meeting place for 4,000 to 5,000 people each month. Many activities take place, such as music, theater groups, production of a newsletter, preparation for festivals, peace groups, study groups, arts and craft activities. The clown, Nögge, devotes much time to creating the type of entertainment that raises important social questions and issues of our time. In addition, there are many visitors who take part in repairing the fabric of the house and other such activities. By working together in this way with the co-workers, warmth and openness is created, so that it is easier to communicate inner thoughts and initiate real dialogue and recognition. Since it is mainly for young people, discussion tends to center upon issues that affect them such as misinformation and lack of understanding of drugs, spiritual movements, problems of housing and accommodation, peace, East-West relations, and so on.

The secret of the Forum lies in the ability of coworkers to listen to the people and not tell them what they should do. They say, "Listening helps to awaken the spirit that lives in every person."

From the beginning of Forum 3 it was also felt that in order to understand and meet people where they are, Forum 3 had to have an open relationship with many kinds of people, political parties and causes. On the other hand, it also believes that along with other characteristic emphases, such as nonviolence, it must have its own firm spiritual identity.

It has also chosen a structure that supports the threefold nature of the human being, that is to say, the will within people's actions, the feelings between people, and the life of thoughts. In Forum 3 they firmly believe that without an inner and outer structure for people's activities, people become ill and confused, for they have no landmarks with which to find their way.

In recent years, many more places like Forum 3 are springing up. Many opportunities for new initiatives are waiting, before every town has its own Life Center, in which people can reconnect with each other and with life in a meaningful way.

Hearthstone Community Association (U.S.A.)
by Ross Jennings

Hearthstone, located in Wilton, New Hampshire (U.S.A.), is a group of eleven families who lease a 92-acre tract of land from the Monadnock Community Land Trust. The 99-year lease pledges the membership of Hearthstone to using and developing the land in an ecologically responsible manner. Hearthstone's relationship to the land trust bears witness to its intention of being a steward to the land and to break the chain of treatment of land as a commodity by removing it from the speculative market.

About twelve years ago, the group that evolved into Hearthstone came together to consider the dilemma posed to the Wilton area by the proposed sale of a farm where biodynamic agriculture was becoming established. While the owner did not wish to see this beginning go to naught, circumstances were forcing him to put the farm on the open market by September 1978, unless some alternative could be found.

That was the question which faced the group gathered on August 17, 1978. As one member of that original group, my expectations were not very high—perhaps an "angel" could be found—but at the very least we would have the satisfaction of having tried to save the farm. As we introduced ourselves, it suddenly became apparent that alongside our concern for the land we had common interests in "community" and individually affordable housing.

Then it was clear that the synthesis of these concerns and interests was leading us to the conclusion that we should buy the farm! In the enthusiasm engendered by this discovery each individual openly shared his or her financial capabilities—(that is, what could be applied to a down payment, what could be contributed to servicing a mortgage). This was a very amazing experience as several of the people gathered didn't know one another previously.

Thus began a process that was to come to mean meeting every week for the first three and a half years. Our individual "obsessions" ranged from homesteading, to windmills, to methane digesters. What became increasingly clear from the outset was the necessity of finding a process that insured that each person's interest could be shared, valued, and respected and that together we had to find the next practical and achievable step. Frequently what appeared to be outer obstacles, such as the complex process for the approval of the project by the town of Wilton, turned out to be a blessing as we were given deadlines to meet, questions to answer, and the responsibility of making our lofty collective vision comprehensible to the "powers that be!" Our work with the town of Wilton is a testament to the value of openness, trust, and clarity. A mutual respect was formed during this process as we sometimes had to compromise.

With the farm saved, the door was open to start a community-building project. The process of building up a shared vision of our "intentionally created neighborhood" was both challenging and fascinating. Our age range (8–80), varied backgrounds (New Hampshire native, Georgists, Parisian cosmopolite) and work experiences (teachers, builders, artists, publisher, retired cop) always made for a lively exchange. After a while, we realized that our real strength lay in our diversity and that as our individual capacities grew to accept and be tolerant of perspectives different from our own the "efficiency" of our work was enhanced. This learning process—stretched over three and a half years of meeting every week—was punctuated by crises that could not be met unless the group was continuously willing to raise its "trust threshold." An important turning point in our work together came in a meeting where we acknowledged that a cornerstone of our work together was to "take on the development of the other." We agreed to be open to one another, and to have the courage to share our feelings and perceptions freely.

One element that has helped us greatly was the inclusion of a short evaluation period as part of each meeting. We began this in the early days of clearing the land as we found it important to set aside time to reflect on the day's work—not only to become more skilful at the tasks but to mend any tears in our social fabric. The opportunity of working together over a prolonged period gave us a refined sense of the nuances of the consensus decision-making process—it's always too slow for one or too fast for the other.

We have found it essential to respect the laws that govern the functioning of our threefold nature as human beings. We come together once or twice a year to look at the question: "Who are we and where are we going?" These "non-business" meetings are important for clearing the air and redefining our work in light of what's possible at any given moment. With a sizeable group, over a long period of time conditions arise that create the challenge of living with a panorama of personal crises. Learning how to objectify and to transform personal upset into opportunity for development for the individual and the group is a goal we have acknowledged as central to our work together.

As the project grew over time, change came in its wake. New members join, new life responsibilities emerge and as one phase of the work together is completed new levels of function must come forth to meet the new challenges. Initially the tasks were fairly straightforward: clearing and stacking wood, building roads, creating a site plan, and working with the town and state authorities. We were very fortunate in these early stages in finding people with necessary professional skills who could provide their services without denying our members the opportunity to contribute. In the end new skills were tapped within the group: a former stage designer produced beautiful site plan drawings, a former teacher dowsed for water, and the responsibility for managing the project became widely shared.

After this beginning phase, individual leaseholders gradually shifted to the awesome task of designing and building their own homes. At present eleven families are living on the land with homes in varying stages of completion. Building a house for most people is a microcosm of the manic-depressive syndrome—wild swings between elation and depression and the discovery that your world horizon has shrunk to a few millimeters' span. This "rite of passage" with other fellow travelers was sometimes a return ticket to sanity.

For the first couple of years our meetings were the only time we saw one another. Now other forms of social contact are gradually evolving. We share festival times together (where individually possible) and include in our meetings time for personal sharing. Purely social occasions—potluck desserts, pancake breakfasts, singing, games, and so on—are a way of meeting prospective new members and to reach out into the larger community.

We have felt from the outset that Hearthstone has a larger purpose than providing low-cost housing opportunities for its members. Much favorable publicity about the project has brought a stream of visitors who are interested in a working example of land trust principles. For the future we envision additional land being cleared for fields and other community buildings. One idea that we are working with would be to create a multifunctional facility: a gathering place for Hearthstone (we no longer easily fit into a single house), a setting for therapeutic work, and a place for workshops and lectures for the public. An indoor swimming pool that would also serve as a passive solar thermal mass is one of our favorite fantasies.

The development costs to date and the purchase monies are repaid through our lease fee, which is also a proportionate share of the taxes, maintenance, insurance, and other running costs. We have so far been able to keep the lease fee affordable and as we add new members our capacity to afford additional development increases. An exciting dimension to the project has been the need to look beyond our membership for development monies. We have sponsored talks on the theme of socially beneficial investment and have worked with organizations such as the Revolving Loan Fund of the Institute for Community Economics.

In summary, I would describe Hearthstone as a living experiment in the relationship of inner and outer development. We have frequently found ourselves faced with decisions whose only reference point was our previous experience. This reminds me of the "oral tradition" and folk wisdom of a tribal society. Our bond, however, is not of blood, but is based on conscious choice. The process together is a continual challenge to exercise our capacities as free individuals who associate to carry out our work for the common good.

Old Plaw Hatch Farm: A Community Endeavor (England)

Another area of great concern to many people is related to the exploitation of the earth and the quality of food that is consumed by many millions of people. Organic and biodynamic farms are experiencing the demand of a rapidly growing market for wholefood products. The price to acquire farmland, however, makes it virtually impossible to buy and develop a farm according to organic or biodynamic principles.

A way out was clearly demonstrated in the development of Old Plaw Hatch Farm in Sharpthorne, England. This farm, farmed since 1970 on biodynamic principles, was privately owned and supplied the local community with unpasteurized milk. The capitalization and running of the farm was a continuous struggle, and in 1980 the farm was offered for sale.

A local land trust, already owning some farmland, was asked to acquire the land on behalf of the community. At a public meeting, consumers living in the local community were asked to buy the farm. The community responded beyond expectation and gifts of over £50,000 were promised. This positive response made it possible for the trustees to acquire low-interest loans through Mercury Provident Society and its sister bank in Germany. They were able to lend a total of £100,000 for a lower interest.

A separate company was formed for the farming activity, the shares of which were held by the same land trust, and the two farmers responsible for the farm were appointed directors of the company. A sum of £32,000 was needed to purchase the livestock of the farm, and Mercury and the German bank were able to make this loan. In order to demonstrate the support of the local community, personal guarantees from members of the community were required to cover at least half of the amount.

Within three years of purchase, the trust received covenants and legacies that enabled it to pay off the greater part of its loan and to carry out substantial improvements to land and buildings. The milk round of unpasteurized milk continues to flourish and a government-sponsored scheme, using local unemployed young people, has opened up neglected areas on the farm to the public for recreational purposes.

The farm, now owned by the local community through the land trust, stands in a unique position to involve the community in many activities on the farm such as festivals, harvesting, and providing a place for the local schools to further the pupils' understanding of nature and agriculture. But the primary gift of the community and others was to remove the land from the property market and make it freely available for the development of biodynamic farming.

Camphill Communities: Curative Education for People with Special Needs[5]

There are five Camphill communities today in the United States and more than fifty throughout the world that provide a successful, alternative approach to caring for and educating mentally retarded children and adults. The Camphill idea began in 1939 when an Austrian pediatrician, Dr. Karl Koenig (1902–1966) and a few followers began a community in Scotland where they shared their lives, their work, and their homes with retarded children.

The Camphill philosophy is rooted in the teachings of Austrian philosopher and educator Rudolf Steiner (1861–1925), who believed that every individual, whether handicapped or not, was a unique spiritual being with freedom, dignity, and a purpose in society. Steiner applied his insights to the practical aspects of daily living such as social organization, farming, medicine, and education, in a branch of philosophy he called "Anthroposophy." It is from his ideas on curative education and community living that Camphill derives it inspiration and way of life.

In the Camphill communities, "special" (the Camphill term for "retarded") children live with staff in normal family structures, attend school with their peers and learn through daily life to experience and appreciate themselves, each other, and the world around them. The programs are for youngsters between the ages of six and twenty-one, and the staff strive to maintain a social environment where normal and retarded people can live together for their mutual benefit. Normally about four to six "special" children live in small houses with several staff members as their family, and each Camphill community has about ten to twenty families. There are also villages for adults in which the same family structure is used.

---

5. Suzanne Schecker, from *New Synthesis Think Tank Papers*, 1987.

Camphill staff believe that what gives self-assurance to a handicapped person is the possibility of belonging to a social community. Harmonious life in a small family is seen as the ground for the development of confidence, trust, and recognition of one's human capabilities. All the Camphill communities attempt to rest on what they call "the three pillars of social life: inner security through regular work; protection through family bonds; and recognition of one's personality by a group of other people."

There is regular work for the "special" children at Camphill communities in workshops where crafts of genuine beauty and quality are produced and sold to the public. In England and America, rag dolls and doll furniture are among the most successful articles made. Care is taken that the same mechanical process is not repeated endlessly in the workshops, so the worker can experience being creatively active. The quality of the experience is considered far more important than productivity. Tools and machines are constructed or adapted for use by people suffering from severe motor disturbances, and every member of a workshop team has insight into the entire process of production. In these ways, people in need of special care can lead a dignified existence where the fruits of their labor are useful and give pleasure to others.

Comprehensive curative education, as expressed by Karl Koenig, is not only a pedagogical and psychological attempt to control children and adults who are handicapped or environmentally disturbed. It also works to help them in such a way that they can regain their own humanity. In its broadest aspects, curative education is not only a science or a practical art, but also a human attitude—an attitude that begins with the growing in the heart of a kind of humility that recognizes the brother or sister in everyone that carries a human countenance. Such humility helps people recognize immediately that they can help only if they are willing to see the helper in their brother or sister—and in themselves, the one who receives help. As Koenig remarked, "Only the help from man to man—the encounter of Ego with Ego—the becoming aware of the other man's individuality without inquiring into his creed, politics, or world conception, but simply the meeting, eye to eye, of two persons creates the curative education that counters in a healing way the threat to our innermost reality."

Blackthorn Garden[6] (England)

The Weald of Kent in the Medway Valley used to be known as the Garden of England. When I grew up there in the forties and fifties, its patchwork landscape was dotted with prolific cherry and apple orchards, cob-nut plats and hop gardens. But in recent decades the sturdy fruit trees have been uprooted, the remaining hop gardens have become tourist attractions, and the agriculture has fallen into the familiar grip of European agribusiness. Yet there are pockets of hope, where pioneering projects can be found. The National Fruit Collection at Brogdale, near Faversham, has recently been saved from the axe, and is now open to the public. The Henry Doubleday Research Association is setting up a new organic garden at Yalding, to be opened in 1993. Furthermore, the most unexpected setting for a biodynamic garden is to be found within the auspices of a medical practice in an otherwise unremarkable suburb of Maidstone.

The Blackthorn Trust, founded in 1985, is concerned with the medical care, rehabilitation and social welfare of patients suffering from serious or chronic illness. It works closely with a National Health Service practice of GPs, offering counseling, art and music therapy, and eurythmy to those in need, regardless of their financial means. This initiative, in itself no mean

---

6. Rose Moore, from *Biodynamics*, Journal of the Biodynamic Farming and Gardening Association.

achievement, is now developing yet another facet, which goes under the name of the Blackthorn Garden. On leased land adjacent to the medical center, it consists of a bakery, a café, and a garden, all of which are open to the public. Patients attending the center are encouraged to visit for lunch or coffee and biscuits, and to buy newly baked bread, freshly harvested flowers and vegetables, bedding plants, and so on.

The aims of Blackthorn Garden are to establish a place of rehabilitation through work for mentally ill people in the local community, and to create a setting for social integration and cultural activity in the Barming district of Maidstone. The project has a staff of three full-time members: Tÿno Voors, director, who administrates, fund-raises, and coordinates with the medical team and all the local bodies concerned with mental health and community care; Hamish Mackay, master baker and formerly a biodynamic farmer in Australia, who is overseeing the bakery and café, and uses Demeter flour brought over from Perry Court Farm near Canterbury; and Chris Hudson the gardener. This team is supported by volunteers who help in the bakery, café, or garden one or more days per week. The volunteers may be patients of the medical center who have been physically ill and need some rehabilitation; or they may be people from the local community who are unemployed, retired, or simply enjoy being involved in such a mutually supportive atmosphere. Staff, volunteers and patients work together (and take coffee, lunch, and tea breaks in the café!), and also have the option on different days of joining study, singing, craft, and eurythmy groups. There is a monthly coworkers meeting, where it has recently been agreed that one third of the monthly income from the proceeds of the work will be shared out between them.

The garden itself has three main aspects, which provide different types of work. There is a landscaped area round the new medical center, complete with its Flowform, which offers an interesting diversion for patients looking out from the waiting-room. The area is still being developed with shrub and tree planting and flower beds. There is a kitchen garden growing vegetables, herbs, and flowers (some for drying); the produce supplies the cafe, and the surplus is sold to customers. Then there is the nursery work, carried out in a large greenhouse with adjacent cold frames. Here coworkers experience the various stages of plant life through sowing, pricking out, and potting on. They produce annual bedding plants, herbs, herbaceous perennials, and houseplants, take cuttings and propagate shrubs, all of which are for sale.

It is amazing that all this has come about in less than a year, transforming an overgrown patch into an oasis of color and interest. The work is being done organically, and biodynamically, as far as is possible where there is no source of BD animal manure, and as yet small amounts of homemade compost. Before he came to Blackthorn, Chris, the gardener, had been trained in conventional commercial horticulture, so he is expert at everything from propagating to path-laying. He also worked for some years in another project with mentally handicapped people, but this is his first experience of biodynamics. He says that the ideas behind it seem like "common sense" to him, but he admits that he was unrealistic in expecting to achieve quick results. It is particularly tricky applying biodynamic methods under the artificial conditions of the greenhouse, which contains plants at all the different stages of growth all year round. However, a start has been made with using the preparations, and the sowing calendar is followed when possible. "It's just not so easy to explain to prospective customers what you are doing when they come across you sitting down stirring a bucket of colorless liquid by hand!"

While time and commitment are needed to consolidate this season's achievements, there are already plans afoot to expand out of Blackthorn's sheltered oasis. With the prospect of extra land available, vegetables may be grown on a larger scale; allotments could be "colonized," or private gardens taken on by more confident coworkers. In any case, this initiative could be a model for others to follow. Next time you visit your "doctor" imagine how it would be to come away with a loaf of bread, 2 pounds of French beans, and a bunch of cornflowers!

Waldorf Schools[7]

The Waldorf School movement encompasses more than 550 schools in 23 countries, many in North America. Founded by Rudolf Steiner, a remarkable Austrian scientist and philosopher born in 1861, the first Waldorf school was established in Stuttgart, Germany, in 1919. It was sponsored by the Waldorf-Astoria factory and financed by a German industrialist who invited Steiner to form the school for children of his employees. Steiner used this opportunity to demonstrate how a school curriculum and teaching methodology could be designed to instill clarity of thought, sensitivity of feeling, and strength of will. Soon other schools were organized in several other countries of Europe and then the U.S. A full range of education is offered for children from ages four to eighteen years.

One of Steiner's major aims was to avoid fragmentation of learning and create a unity of experience—a balance among the sciences, the humanities, and the arts. He also eliminated the typical school timetable that jumps from one subject to another with staccato transitions, in favor of the so-called "main lesson." This is a two-hour period each morning, devoted to one subject for from three to five weeks at a time. A learning process, he believed, could then be built with a growing sense of discovery from day to day by concentrating on one subject of significance. Waldorf education is designed to affect the conscious, the semiconscious, and the unconscious life of the child. It is assumed that only so much can be

---

7. Beldon Paulson, from *New Synthesis Think Tank Papers*, 1987.

learned intellectually; real feeling for a subject takes root through music, painting of related pictures, recitations, and other artistic and cultural activities.

Waldorf education has three essential phases, which relate to the needs and capabilities of the child at different periods of growth. The first seven years, basically the preschool period, are a time when the child learns a great deal through imitation, mimicking not only the sounds of speech and movements of people and machines, but also the attitudes and values of parents and peers. The kindergarten then becomes a warm, loving, and secure home, where free play and fantasy are facilitated.

The second phase encompasses the first eight grades. Literature and language are crucial during these years. For example, in the first grade fairy tales are narrated, when the child can meet the forces of good and evil in imaginative ways. In grade two legends and fables are told; in the third grade the story of creation. The fourth grade includes the dramatic world of Norse mythology. The fifth grade is a threshold; it is when the study of history begins, one of the central subject areas in Waldorf education. History is seen as a mosaic of facts, but is also a philosophical process that involves the web of interaction of two central themes of the twentieth century: the idea of nationalism and the concept of the unity of humankind. Cultivation of the cultural roots of identity and sense of place are complementary to the "globalness of human affairs" and the deeper layers of meaning in history and in ourselves.

During grades one to eight the acquisition of literacy and mathematics and information is constantly interrelated with the child's imaginative faculties, which are drawn out through poetry, drawing, drama, music, cultural activities, and practical activities such as carpentry and knitting. The child is, in essence, an "artist," and awe and feelings and sense of discovery are built into the subject matter. For example, in geography the teacher may seek to convey artistically, descriptively, dramatically the picture of the climatic zones of Africa—the burning dry Sahara or clammy rain forest of the Guinea Coast.

The third phase is high school, grades nine to twelve, when the ideal of adulthood is imaged: thoughtful, self-possessed, considerate, strong-minded, warmhearted. By the last two years pupils begin to see the world as "the womb of humankind," feeling a part of the planet, responsible for it, and dependent on it.

Much thought and effort is spent by Waldorf teachers in faculty meetings. Because Waldorf schools are independent of the state, the teachers, referred to as the College of Teachers, share in managing the school, from development of educational policies within the broad guidelines of all Waldorf education, to organizing the human and material resources, including finding funds. Although all Waldorf schools are part of the international movement, united by dedication to a common curriculum, each school is independently managed and has its own distinct characteristics. Parents become actively involved in fund-raising and in close and total school support. Teacher training programs exist in a variety of localities, including Sunbridge College in Spring Valley, N.Y. and Rudolf Steiner College in Fair Oaks, CA.

The Threefold Community in Chestnut Ridge, New York (U.S.A.)

In 1923, a group of people living in New York City formed the Threefold Group to study and work with Rudolf Steiner's ideas, and to help plant the seeds of Anthroposophy on American soil. They opened a vegetarian restaurant near Carnegie Hall that became a popular meeting place for artists. In 1926, they bought a thirty-two acre farm in Spring Valley, New York (now Chestnut Ridge), to raise biodynamic produce for the restaurant and to establish a conference, vacation, and educational center. 1933 saw the first of many summer conferences to be held at "Threefold Farm."

Over the years, Threefold added property and activities that reflect three ongoing concerns: biodynamic agriculture, social renewal, and education. The land now harbors the following organizations and initiatives, that together form a growing community of works serving the human being from childhood to old age.

- GREEN MEADOW WALDORF SCHOOL, founded in 1951, has four hundred students, from nursery through twelfth grade. It has a reputation for academic excellence, and actively supports the Waldorf education movement world-wide. Many Sunbridge College students observe classes and do practice teaching at Green Meadow, guided by its teachers.

- EURYTHMY SPRING VALLEY offers a full four-year training and a postgraduate year in eurythmy, a performing art founded by Rudolf Steiner as a spiritual renewal for the art of movement. Eurythmy is also used in education and therapy. Eurythmy Spring Valley's performing group performs nationally and abroad.

- SUNBRIDGE COLLEGE's full-time adult education programs include an Orientation Year, Waldorf Teacher Training and Early Childhood Education, and a Master's Program in Waldorf Education. Part-time options include the Evening Program, an Associate Early Childhood Program, and courses in Waldorf School Administration and Community Development.

- THE MAIN HOUSE serves home-cooked lunches in its dining room, using biodynamic and organic foods whenever possible.

- HOLDER HOUSE is a recently completed 40-unit student residence and conference facility.

- THE HUNGRY HOLLOW FOOD CO-OP sells biodynamic produce and organic and other whole food products to members and customers. It's also a focal point for community life, offering hot coffee and fresh baked goods from the Main House bakery.

■ THE FELLOWSHIP COMMUNITY, founded in 1961, is an intergenerational community serving the elderly. Life at the Fellowship is active, with a biodynamic garden, print shop, candle shop, and a growing practice in anthroposophically extended medicine.

■ THE RUDOLF STEINER FOUNDATION is a financial services organization for the Anthroposophical Society in America, facilitating financial transactions between donors, lenders, and receivers. Interest-bearing loan accounts are available to individuals and organizations who wish to participate in the growth of anthroposophical initiatives. The Foundation has close links with many initiatives in Threefold.

■ WELEDA, INC. Weleda USA makes medicines for use in anthroposophically extended medical practices. It is part of a worldwide organization developed after Rudolf Steiner's first medical course in 1921. Weleda Pharmacy at Threefold compounds and dispenses prescription medications and offers a variety of body care products and natural and homeopathic remedies.

■ ENVISION ASSOCIATES is an organization and community development consultancy group serving a wide variety of clients in the nonprofit and profit sectors.

The Community Development Resource Association (South Africa)

The Community Development Resource Association (CDRA) was established in 1987 in response to the need to build the capacity of nongovernmental organizations (NGOs) and community-based organizations (CBOs) in southern Africa. CDRA is itself a not-for-profit NGO based in Cape Town, South Africa.

NGOs and CBOs have grown from small beginning to emerge as important players in the development process in South Africa. CDRA's prime objective is to contribute to the growth of civil society in South Africa through the provision of organization development (OD) support services to these organizations. We believe that strengthening their organizational capacity will contribute toward community development which in turn will help the growth of civil society.

CDRA understands organizational capacity to be the ability of an organization to:

- act in an effective and productive way and competently reflect on, learn from, and improve its activities
- maintain and develop an organizational climate that is reflective, provides space and meaning for staff, and that has a sense of collective responsibility and potential for growth
- respond and adapt to its changing environment, proactively plan for the future, and understand its development activities within the wider societal context.

CDRA works toward strengthening these abilities by providing consultancy services at the request of client organizations and developing and running various training courses.

Townsend and Bottum Inc.
Continuity Planning and a New Ownership Form (U.S.A.)

Bill Bottum is a thoughtful and gregarious man in his late sixties. He had joined Townsend and Bottum as a young engineer when the organization was led by his father. By 1979 he had been the chief executive officer for some time. The company was facing a changing market in the construction industry and he was aware that new strategies, a new ownership form, and succession planning were required if Townsend and Bottum was to successfully enter the 1980s. In March 1979 he called together the top managers of the company for a long-term strategic planning meeting. The results of this meeting were to be dramatic over the next five years, leading to a process of change in the company's direction, in relationships, in structure, and in the form of ownership.

Seen from the outside, this change process in Townsend and Bottum comprised five main areas. One was the focusing of the company's mission and values—or its corporate culture. Townsend and Bottum in 1985 developed a T. and B. Mission Statement that stressed serving the real needs of clients with absolute integrity. It also noted that the values within the organization were to be commensurate with the tenets of the world's great religions, and that the organization and its employees were to be a "witness, and an example, of human and spiritual values to employees, clients, business and community."

A second area of change was in the quality of relationships. The company's objective was to "create a climate of openness, sincerity, integrity, and trust" capable of permeating the organization and its internal and external relationships. The company took a number of steps toward this objective, beginning in 1974 with communication skills training. Status symbols separating employees were removed. Over one hundred employees took part in team building and communication workshops designed and carried out by an external consulting firm. Team building and conflict resolution workshops were also extended to relationships with client organizations so that joint problem solving orientations were fostered. The concept of leadership was examined and use was made of Robert K. Greenleaf's book *Servant Leadership—A Journey into the Nature of Legitimate Power and Greatness*. Greenleaf stresses that effective leaders of the future will be motivated by a desire to serve rather than a drive for power and status. In addition, employees were encouraged to reflect on their own styles of working, through using a Life Styles Inventory, developed by Human Synergistics in Plymouth, Michigan. The idea of being an effective model rather than a moralizer was central to the process of creating greater trust and cooperation within the organization.

A third area of development was the restructuring and decentralization of the company. In 1978 T. and B. consisted of one main company, Townsend and Bottum, with 664 employees; Project Management Associates with 31 employees; and Jilco Inc. with 28 employees. By 1985 it consisted of fourteen decentralized groups, which included the "not-for-profit" Servant Leader Center as the research and educational component of T. and B.

The fourth area of major change was finding an ownership form which would guarantee the continuity of the company. After much research a Capital Fund form was chosen. This meant that private shareholders were bought out and that a board of trustees would hold the company's assets for the company's present and future employees.

A last question for the organization was passing the reins of responsibility to a new generation of managers. This process is still underway with Bill Bottum having resigned as chief executive officer and functioning as a mentor and advisor to the new top management team.

The Townsend and Bottum experience, described in outline form, is beginning to serve as an inspiration to other businesses who seek to become more service-oriented, human, moral, and effective modern industries. It is a heartwarming effort to bring new values and forms into economic life. A summary of key concepts is added.

For more information write to:

The Servant Leader Center, 2245 South State Street,
P.O. Box 1368, Ann Arbor, MI 48106, U.S.A.

SOME KEY CONCEPTS

1. Neutralization of Capital—Capital as a working tool for each generation of managers.
2. Portion of increases in capital goes to current managers. Balance accumulates.
3. Recognize individual differences in talent, capability, and business judgement.
4. Cooperation and brotherhood in economic sphere.
5. Equality in rights sphere.
6. Liberty and freedom in spiritual activity—encourage growth and development.
7. Self-transcending motivation toward benefit for all mankind.

Future:

8. Producer's income diminishes when losses occur, thus stabilizing employment.

Addressed by:

1. Continuity Plan that eliminates common stock.
   Governance by trustees.
2. Income Distribution Units (I.D.U.) Program shares profits - bonus pool.
3. Compensation and I.D.U. Systems reward performance. Trustees not elected.
4. Team-Building programs including clients. Communication skill training.
5. Equal opportunity. Eliminate status symbols. Participative management.
6. By-Laws provide for religious freedom. Life Styles Inventory for development.
7. Servant Leader Center.

Future:

8a. Spun off entities self-adjust pay to respond to market.
8b. Explore application to T & B Family of Companies.

Diaperaps (U.S.A.)

Diaperaps Ltd. was founded in 1984 by Rachael Flug and Abraham Entin, a husband-wife team who still own and operate the company. Rachael is president and CEO, while Abraham concentrates on sales and marketing.

The company was founded out of a desire to achieve "right livelihood." Both partners felt a commitment to cotton diapers based on a recognition that babies are better served by having natural fibers next to their skin, and also based upon a recognition of the environmental consequences of single-use products in general, and diapers in particular.

The goal of the company was to produce and market a *mass-market* product that would make using cotton diapers easy and convenient. Low cost, as well as ease of use and treatment, were key elements in achieving that end. This has remained the focus of our energy through the years.

As well as manufacturing a product that helps parents make an ecologically responsible diapering choice, the company has also paid a great deal of attention to the environmental consequences of its own operation. It examines the processes by which its components are manufactured, trying to achieve the lowest impact in this area that is possible. In addition, the company has been recognized for its leadership in packaging reduction efforts, and uses recycled materials for its packaging. Finally, the company has had internal recycling programs (as well as waste reduction programs) in effect for many years.

The result is that Diaperaps Ltd. is a "certified Green Business," according to Co-op America, which audits and grants this certification. The company is also a founding member of Business for Social Responsibility and is committed to a regular program of charitable giving.

Internally, the company has always maintained a policy of providing health benefits for all employees, regardless of "rank." We have also tried to maintain flexibility of scheduling to accommodate parents with young children, nursing mothers, and so on. As a small company, this is not always an easy thing to accomplish, but it remains a company goal.

Overall, a primary goal of the company has been to raise consciousness among the public about the products they use and the consequences of those products. It was, and is, our hope that, by dealing with new parents, at the beginning of a new cycle of life and responsibility, we can introduce new products and ways of looking at issues that will have a positive impact on the lives of the individuals involved and on the society as a whole.

As part of this process, we are moving toward the development of new products that will utilize and promote the usage of organically grown, ecologically sustainable fibers and manufacturing. We hope to be able to support the spread of biodynamic and organic agriculture through this venture, by increasing demand (and demonstrating increased demand) for products that are grown and manufactured in socially responsible ways.

ADDRESSES OF INITIATIVES DESCRIBED

Forum 3
Gymnasiumstrasse 21, Stuttgart, Germany

Plaw Hatch Farm
Sharpthorne, West Sussex RH19 4JL, England

Waldorf Schools
Association of Waldorf Schools in North America (AWSNA), 3911 Bannister Road, Fair Oaks, CA 95628, U.S.A.

Steiner Schools Fellowship, Orlingbury House, Lewes Road, Forest Row, East Sussex RH18 5AA, England

Association of Rudolf Steiner Schools in Australia, P.O. Box 82, Dural 2158, Australia

Blackthorn Garden
Blackthorn Trust, Maidstone, Kent, England

Hearthstone Community Association
Wilton, NH 03086, U.S.A.

Diaperaps
9760 Owensmouth Avenue, Chatsworth, CA 91311, U.S.A.

Camphill Foundation
Pughtown Road, P.O. Box 290, Kimberton, PA 19442, U.S.A.

ARTA, Life and Work Community
Krakelingweg 25, 3707 HP Zeist, Holland

Townsend and Bottum
2245 South State Street, P.O. Box 1368, Ann Arbor, MI 48106, U.S.A.

The Door
555 Broome Street, New York, NY 10013, U.S.A.

Threefold Educational Foundation and School
285 Hungry Hollow Road, Chestnut Ridge, NY 10977, U.S.A.

Gifts of Love
P.O. Box 906, Simsbury, CT 06070, U.S.A.

Enabling Development: A Tribute to Colleagues

This book has drawn extensively on the experiences of a network of individuals and groups committed to human, social, and economic renewal who have been inspired by the work of the Austrian educator and philosopher, Rudolf Steiner (1861– 1925). A part of this network is banks and financial institutions who help individuals and institutions find a more conscious relationship to money. These include:

The Mercury Provident Society Ltd.
   Orlingbury House, Lewes Road, Forest Row,
   East Sussex RH18 5AA, England

Triodosbank NV
   Stationslaan 4, Postbus 55, 3700 AB Zeist, Holland

GLS Gemeinschaftsbank eG
   Oskar-Hoffman Strasse 25, 4630 Bochum, Germany

Rudolf Steiner Foundation
   RD 1, Box 147A, Chatham, NY 12037, U.S.A.

Southern Cross Capital Exchange
   88 Lawton View Road, Wentworth Falls, N.S.W. 2782, Australia

Prometheus Foundation
   P.O. Box 1397, Hastings, New Zealand

A second field of activity that informs our work is that of "Lifeways," which is both the title of a successful book[8] and a description of a growing field of work in areas of human development, family life, parenting, and gender questions. As a mother in the U.S.A. wrote:

> I am from a working class background. My mother
> worked and so did her mother. I have three small chil-
> dren, and I do not know where or how to start to build a

---

8. Davy, Gudrun and Bons Voors, *Lifeways* (Stroud, U.K.: Hawthorn Press, 1983), Volume 2 is now in progress.

family life at home. I have chosen to be a mother, and, boy, it's the hardest job I've ever taken on. I am just about drowning, but I am still determined to become a good mother and a good wife. The book *Lifeways* is my lifebelt. I underline things which I find helpful. I realize I am not the only one who finds it difficult. I am reading all these wonderful suggestions and ways to look at things. Last Christmas was the first time we made things instead of buying presents. It was very special.

Contact Addresses for Lifeways Groups:
Jennifer Brooks Quinn
Center for Life Studies, Sunbridge College
260 Hungry Hollow Road, Chestnut Ridge, NY 10977

Gudrun Davy
11 Hoathley Hill, West Hoathley, Sussex RH194GL

Central to our work are our colleagues who work as teachers and advisors in the field of organization and community development around the world. Many of them are members of the Association for Social Development and bring a conscious spiritual perspective to the work of helping individuals, groups, and organizations build effective work communities.

ENGLISH-SPEAKING EDUCATIONAL INITIATIVES

Centre for Social Development, Emerson College
Old Plaw Hatch House, Sharpthorne, West Sussex RH19 4JL, England

Institute for Social Development
P.O. Box 350, Roseville, N.S.W. 2069, Australia

The Waldorf Administration and Development Program
Sunbridge College, 260 Hungry Hollow Road, Chestnut Ridge, NY 10977, U.S.A.

CONSULTANCY GROUPS

Envision Associates
285 Hungry Hollow Road, Chestnut Ridge, NY 10977, U.S.A.

Growing Edge
3 Elm Street, Peterborough, NH 03458, U.S.A.

Transform
Suite 55–66, High Street, Sheffield S12 GE, England

Rubicon Associates
3 Ashdown Farm Cottage, Forest Row, East Sussex,
RH185 I2, England

Catalyst-Hammond
4 Topham Crescent, Richmond Hill, Ontario L4C9G2,
Canada

Trigon
8042 Graz, St. Peter Hauptstrasse 208, Austria

Social Ecology Associates, Graeme Harvey
23 Willunga Crescent, Forestville, N.S.W. 2087, Australia

Social Ekology Associates
Kärralundsgatan 55, S–41656 Göteborg, Sweden

Social Ecology Associates
37 Summer Street, Ponsonby, Aukland I, New Zealand

N.P.I., Institute for Organization Development
Valckenboschlaan 8, 3703 CR Zeist, Holland

*B.G.O., Beraterverband für Gegenwartsfragen und Organisation-
sentwickelung*
Nägelseestrasse 23, 7800 Freiburg, Germany

Adigo
Ave Doria 164, Sao Paulo, SP 04635 Brazil

Christophorus
Estrada do Iacequava, 5500–04870 Santa Amano, Sao Paulo,
Brazil

CDRA, Community Development Resource Association
6 Beach Road, Woodstock, Cape Town 7925, South Africa

ABOUT THE AUTHORS

CHRISTOPHER SCHAEFER, Ph.D. was a founding member of Social Ecology Associates and a cofounder of the Centre for Social Development at Emerson College in England. He has worked in the fields of organization and community development for twenty years. During this time he has worked with a variety of clients in England, Germany, and the United States, including Kimberton Waldorf School, Ford Motor Company, Seneca College, Lamb Studios, and many other groups. Prior to his work with Social Ecology Associates he taught Social Science at the Massachusetts Institute of Technology. He is currently a faculty member of Sunbridge College in Spring Valley, New York, and the director of their Waldorf School Administration and Community Development Program. He is also a founding member of Envision Associates, an organization development group in North America, co-Director of the Center for Organization and Community Development, and is the director of the Blackthorn Garden.

TŸNO VOORS, lecturer at the Centre for Social Development, Emerson College in England, he worked as a consultant on questions of community and organization development for many years. He has been closely involved with Mercury Provident Society Ltd. in England and Triodos NV in Holland—two new banking initiatives on approaches to handling money. He also worked for many years as a management consultant with the N.P.I. Institute for Organization Development in Holland. He lives with his wife and three children in Sussex, England.

WARREN ASHE is a founder director (1974) of Mercury Provident and is an active board member. He is particularly interested in the problems of associations, policies, and incomes. Born in New York in 1935, he came to England at the age of sixteen and has had a long career in teaching and school administration on the financial side. He teaches humanities subjects in Michael Hall School, Sussex.

STEPHEN BRIAULT, M.A. was born in England and educated in London and Cambridge. He worked for several years in therapeutic communities and later in educational administration and finance. After a period of involvement in refugee resettlements, he trained at the Centre for Social Development where he is now a member of the teaching staff. He is also active as a trainer and consultant for diverse organizations and a founding partner in Rubicon, an organization development consultancy group.

ROY BUNCE was for many years a minister and educator before moving into fund-raising and development work. He was a founding member of Partners in Community Dialogue, a development consultancy organization and is presently active in public relations and fund-raising work.